Religion and Judaism

From A Different Perspective

Written By

Rachel Angel-Sussman

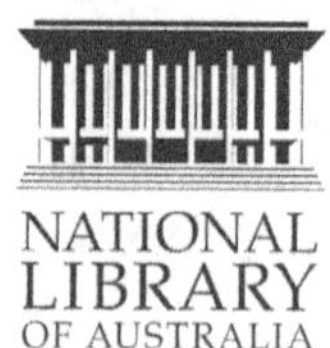

A catalogue record for this book is available from the National Library of Australia

Publisher:
ASPG (Australian Self Publishing Group)
P.O. Box 159, Calwell, ACT Australia 2905
Email: publishaspg@gmail.com
http://www.inspiringpublishers.com

National Library of Australia Cataloguing-in-Publication entry

Author: Angel-Sussman, Rachel

Title: **RELIGION AND JUDAISM:** *From A Different Perspective*/Rachel Angel-Sussman

ISBN: 978-0-6451228-9-3

Dedicated to Humanity,

To the essential beauty, goodness, and light that is the Source of all life and is within all life including each of us.

The beauty, goodness, and light that is who we and all life really are, and that gives rise to, and is at the core of all religions.

May we allow this beauty, goodness, and light shine once more within us and lead us forward.

(Rachel Angel-Sussman)

The fault dear Brutus
Is not in our stars
But in ourselves,
That we are the underlings

(In *"Julius Caesar"* By W. Shakespeare)

Contents

Foreword 7

From The Author 10

PART 1: Religion From A Different Perspective 15

Chapter 1: The Origin and Purpose of Religion........................16

Chapter 2: There is Nothing New Under the Sun 39

Chapter 3: Why does Evil Exists? 42

Chapter 4: One Truth – Why Different Religions?.........................49

Chapter 5: The Pitfalls of The 'Package Deal'........................55

Chapter 6: Offering Vs Imposing.......................................64

Chapter 7: In Conclusion..68

Chapter 8: The Next Step..71

PART 2: Judaism From A Different Perspective 77

Chapter 9: The Story of Judaism and
       its Underlying Message.................................78

Chapter 10: The Jewish People & Judaism's
          'Package Deal' 113

Chapter 11: Judaism and The Jewish People in the World..........123

Chapter 12: Relationship to The Source of Life (God).................. 142

Chapter 13: Family, Marriage and Gender Relationships............150

Chapter 14: Dietary Laws 159

Chapter 15: Times and Seasons 178

Epilogue... 195

Acknowledgement 199

Bibliography 200

Foreword

T he week I completed *Religion and Judaism From A Different Perspective* I came across an article written by Nikki Gemmell in "The Australian Weekend Magazine".

The article moved me because it re-enforced my own journey and expressed what so many, including myself, feel about religion. It also expressed what motivated me to write this book.

I thank Nikki for allowing me to include the article as an introduction to *Religion and Judaism From A Different Perspective* and I hope that this book will provide some answers to the dilemmas raised in this article and shared by so many...

Extract from 'Outside The Box' by Nikki Gemmell in the *Australian Weekend Magazine*, May 30-31, 2020:

"Maybe we are ready for new ways of faith.

Down the rabbit hole of lockdown I find myself turning again and again to the world of ultra-Orthodox Jew. New York's Williamsburg to be precise, with the bracing Netflix series *Unorthodox*, and Jerusalem's Geula in the gentle *Shtisel*, both filmed mainly in Yiddish and rich with glorious difference. I am going full niche here in the Covid streaming tastes, diving deeply into worlds I know next to nothing about and absolutely loving it.

Both series are about various individuals chafing against the bindings of their organised religion, worlds that always seem so destructive to those inclined towards the fiercely individual. Yet what if the mavericks are deeply spiritual too? Where do they go? Can an intersection between the two somehow work, without deep unhappiness on either side?

Christianity at its rigid side extremities is like ultra-Orthodox Judaism in its demands for strict obedience, in its sidelining of females in the upper echelons of leadership. Yet how does organized religion cater for the spiritually minded who also happen to be deep thinkers – the questioners, the rebels, those chafing against strict traditional gender demarcations?

Organised religion demands obedience, a submission to dogma, an adherence to codes often at odd with modern life. Does it ever willingly accommodate those who say, 'I may want your teachings, but there's something a bit whiffy about how you go about it in terms of individual freedoms, because you seem to be vanishing the thinking individual in the process'. What of those of faith who may be revolted by the fallible, all too human leaders helming their religion?

What would religion look like with women leaders at its centre? Where is the church that treats us as equals in the upper echelons of leadership, rather than as convenient dogsbodies to hand out religious texts and turn on the urns? The righteous women of *Shtisel* and *Unorthodox*, seem little more than glorified baby-making machines.

Rachel Angel-Sussman..9

Would an organised religion helmed by women have tolerated the behaviour of paedophile clergy? Would female leaders have acted differently? What would an organised religion developed and helmed by females look like if their own interpretations of the Bible became accepted gospel?

(....)

'I still believed in God, but I didn't believe in church,' writer lyz Lenz wrote in her memoir *God Land*. 'Because I could not imagine life outside the womb of my faith, I struggled inside its limitations. I thought there would always be room for me. But the reality was, there was only room for me if I made myself smaller and smaller and smaller, until I disappeared'.

Unorthodox and *Shtisel* both look at individuals battling against the codes of the religions that bind them. What of the spiritual faith-questioners – do they go it alone? Do they really need a tight religious structure around them? Maybe now, with the world so upended, we're ready for new, looser ways of faith too. For those who have what they need in their hearts; who veer towards wonder".

From the Author

Religion And Judaism From A Different Perspective is written for each of us whether we chose to embrace and practice a particular religion, to reject a particular religion or the whole notion of 'religion', or to simply accept its existence.

The book's second part focuses on Judaism – the religion to which I was born – however, the principles of exploration, the reflections and the messages apply to all religions (and non-religion), and to all of us as human beings.

Readers who have an aversion to the word 'God' need realize that 'God' is simply an archetypal name/image used to define and symbolize the Source of Life however this Source is perceived and experienced. Feel free to replace 'God' with your perception and experience of the Source of Life – be it Life Force, Universal Energy, Universe, Nature, Energy Field, the Big Bang, or whatever else feels true.

We live in a world where so much destruction and suffering is being (and has been) inflicted in the name of God and religion and equally in the name of anti-God and anti-religion (atheism). Little wonder so many have given up on religion, reject it or even its mere concept, see it as the source of all evil, and believe that without religion our world would be a peaceful, loving, harmonious and free heaven.

I too believed so until I set out on a personal journey.

The motivation for this journey was not to find the truth about religion but the need and desire to heal within, to discover the truth of my being and to come 'Home'. However, it resulted also with realizing the truth about 'religion'.

It cleared the 'mud' obscuring religion and unveiled its 'diamond'.

It laid the ground for my reconciliation with 'Religion', particularly with Judaism, and it set me free to listen within and make choices on my behalf and to give others the same freedom.

It allowed me to finally hear the music - A music that I want and feel a responsibility to share in *Religion and Judaism From A Different Perspective*.

Till I set on this personal journey I was 'lost' without recognizing it, and I am not alone. When it comes to religion 'being lost' wears many 'unrecognizable faces':

- Some may adhere rigidly and often blindly to a certain religion and its prescribed practices. This tends to come hand in hand with a rejection of other religions and their prescribed practices. They may not consider themselves 'lost' but rather 'enlightened' – for they are the passionate holder of 'the one and only' true religion, are they not?
- Some may reject the whole concept of religion - all religions and practices. They definitely do not consider themselves 'lost' but rather 'modern', 'enlightened' and free of

> a 'primitive need', of the 'source of evil', of a misguided 'crutch' that is nothing but an 'opiate' for the people' – for isn't religion all these?
> - Other may flounder between denial and belief, perplexed, and confused. They too may not consider themselves 'lost' but rather find comfort in avoidance under the banner that 'religion is really not an important issue for them'.

Only a few have intentionally or 'accidently' journeyed to unveil the 'Diamond'; to realize that we are fully responsible for the demise and that it was time to stop blaming religion and God and start unveiling the truth of our hearts and spirits and find a new kind of faithfulness in love and freedom that leaves room to recognize and embrace the kaleidoscope of truths within many hearts and spirits.

Religion and Judaism From A Different Perspective differs from other written work about religion(s). It does not aim to compare religions to each other, to 'philosophize' about religion, nor to prove (or disprove) the 'truth' of the factual/ historical events upon which they were founded.

Religion and Judaism From A different Perspective is written from inner experience and realization, from a free and peaceful place within where truth simply recognizes itself. It aims to support readers to realize what religion really is and how it can 'go wrong'. It invites each reader to set out on a journey in which "Faithfulness must turn into betrayal first, then betrayal turns into faith, then we can be part of the truth" (Brother David Stein-Rast, in the *Mystical Core of Organized Religion*, New Realities VolX, No 4, March/April 1990, pp 35-37).

This journey is more than discovering the truth about religion.

It allows us to re-discover our human soul.

It sets us free to choose for ourselves while respectfully recognizing choices made by others.

It allows us to regain individual and collective inner and outer peace.

It facilitates hearing the music. And only when we finally hear the music can we begin to:

- Replace blindness, hate, destruction, and inflicting suffering in the name of religion and God with tolerance, compassion, and unity.
- See with clarity that although paths may differ, at their core the same diamond shines.
- Heal ourselves, the collective consciousness and inevitably, our world.

This is my prayer and hope....

Part 1:
Religion From A Different Perspective

Be Still, Look Within
You will discover that
The Truth Simply Is
And you will Hear the music. . .

(Rachel Angel-Sussman)

Chapter 1:
The Origin and Purpose of Religion

Religion cannot be addressed without pondering why do we humans have religions. No other living species worries about religion, why do we? What is the purpose of religion?

Karl Marx stated that religion is the opium of the people. Similarly, Atheists often claim religion to be an expression of a 'primitive need', or 'a crutch' for those who are weak and cannot cope with life.

Are these claims true?

Friedrich Nietzsche words provide the perfect answer to all these claims:

And those who were seen dancing
Were thought to be insane
By those who could not
Hear the music

It is not surprising that those who are dancing are thought to be insane because unfortunately in today's world to a lesser or greater extend across all religions, it is the 'noise' not the music that the dancers are dancing to and it is the 'noise' not the music that the observers hear, see, and understandably reject.

If we are to understand religion and hear its music and message, we must first hear the music of our human soul. We must re-discover the nature of life and who we really are as humans and as individuals. This requires an inner journey and only when we embark on it, the mystery of religion unfolds, and we begin to hear its music and unveil its dance with both its beauty and its lurking pitfalls.

The realizations resulting from my inner journey were encapsulated in my first book *To Life - A Journey of Home Coming and Re-Discovering Our Self and Our Humanity*. As this journey is not only at the core of personal growth, but also at the core of understanding religion, hearing its music, and realizing what is needed to turn around the wheels of our troubled world, glimpsing its essence must be the starting point for *Religion and Judaism From A different Perspective*.

Embarking on an Inner Journey

There are many reasons why we may embark on an inner journey:

- We may be seeking healing and wholeness – maybe we need to heal from past events that continue to contaminate our present; maybe we feel 'blocked' or out of alignment with ourselves or the life we live; maybe we sense there is more to us, something true and deep within for which we long; or maybe we feel that the present is 'collapsing' on us.

- Sometimes we 'stumble' on an inner journey – maybe an inner or outer experience, a realization, or an 'Aha' moment has left us with a new wonder, a new understanding that acts as a magnet from which a journey begins.
- We may be simply curious or seeking answers to some questions that life poses us.

There are also different frames of heart and mind in which we travel. While at times we embark on a journey by our own accord, willingly and intentionally, other times, we may resist till we are 'pushed from behind' and we may even 'kick and scream' the whole way...

Whatever prompted us to embark on the journey and whatever the frame of heart and mind in which we travel, if we follow the journey to its conclusion, we will all arrive to what is defined as 'Self-realization' or 'Enlightenment'. What it means is that –

- We come to realize the nature of existence and who we really are as human beings and as individuals.
- We come to see the interconnectedness and the Oneness of all existence.
- We gain an insight into the mystery of ourselves and all life.

We therefore see with more authentic, loving, and wise eyes and can choose to live from a new place - from our Inner Home. This is the purpose of an inner journey and these are the truths that we must at least glimpse if we are to truly live, be whole and at peace with ourselves, others, all living things. They are also the truths shinning at the core of all religions.

Many have embarked on an inner journey before us, many are travelling with us, and many will travel after us. While we must each travel in our own way and while each of our journeys will take its own twists and turns, we also share common paths and road signs. I have come to realize there are two paths to journey: from *within-out* and from *without-in*.

Unveiling these two paths aims to facilitate experiencing these truths.

Readers are encouraged to 'sense' and 'experience' the words and process rather than only 'understand' them intellectually. 'Sensing' and 'experiencing' facilitates its own deep understanding and realization.

Journeying from Within- Out...

The journey from within tends to be a response to a call to seek healing and wholeness. It is an inward journey of unveiling the inner layers to realize who we really are, the interconnectedness and oneness of all there is, and the Source of all there is.

It often begins when we feel out of ease and recognize a 'broken' alignment between how we present ourselves - the 'Persona' mask we wear - and how we are inside - the 'internal Me'.

For example, while we may present ourselves as self-assured and confident there is a growing awareness that within we feel insecure, doubtful and fearful; while we may present ourselves as loving, caring, accepting and grateful there is a growing awareness that within we feel resentment, anger, rejection and rebellion; and so on.

Sometimes we wear the masks so well that we fool ourselves. But one day we may notice, or maybe this 'broken alignment' becomes too painful to bear. When this happens, we hopefully find a way to gather courage, be honest with ourselves, and give ourselves permission to feel and experience what really is within and begin to remove the mask.

The purpose of removing the 'Persona' mask off is not to project or express inner doubts, fears, insecurities, anger, resentment etc outwardly. It is to develop an awareness and to honestly acknowledge and explore the inner world - the 'inner Me' – see it for what it is and begin a process of healing and growth. The result will be *Honest, Loving, Wise* and *Free* expression because going within and allowing this 'inner Me' be and unveil leads to deeper discoveries...

We realize that the 'inner Me' under the 'Persona' mask is to a great extent another 'mask', another layer of 'personality' created by our past choices with which we now identify and call 'Me'. These choices may have been made consciously, semi consciously, or unconsciously. They are established patterns of being and responding, and an accumulated collection of beliefs and stories about ourselves, others, life etc which we have either told ourselves or have absorbed from our parents, teachers, country, culture etc and have taken on as truth. We come to see that it is we who created this 'Me' intending to either express, or defend, or hide what lies beneath.

I call this 'Me' the 'Psychological-self', and if we remain still, what lies beneath it begins to unveil... It often requires a willingness to move through a number of 'layers' of established patterns, or of beliefs and stories, to eventually realize that at their core lies a 'collection' of 'instinctive' drives, of innate needs and desires, of potential gifts and challenges, and a vast personal and collective genetic and evolutionary heritage. They are the 'inner cards' handed to us and if we gather the courage to –

- Honestly, lovingly, and wisely see how we have treated ourselves and these 'inner cards', the choices we have made in relation to them and why.
- Own these 'inner cards' with a wise and loving acceptance and exercise our freedom to either make new choices in relation to them or keep old choices.
- Realize that our choices are never locked or fixed and that the door must always be left open to review them. What we said 'no' to yesterday we may say 'yes' to today and vice versa, what we chose to 'extend' yesterday we may choose to 'limit' today and vice versa.

A new and deeper alignment will begin to take place between 'Me' (the 'Psychological-self') and these 'Inner Cards' and we will begin to find true healing, growth, and freedom.

However, the journey is still not complete and if we stay on the path, we will make another discovery...

Alongside these 'inner cards' we will begin to notice 'something else': A flowing yet still Inner Presence deep within that is aware, essentially free, innately intelligent, creative, loving, and wise, and attributed with all the qualities deriving from love[1]; an Inner Presence that shines and radiates within us and through us in

---

[1] Many qualities derive from 'love' - kindness, compassion, honesty, integrity, courage, playfulness and so on. Throughout this text, while 'love' will be used when referring to the nature of Inner Presence, or of Source, it extends to encompass all these qualities.

its own unique beauty and is capable of guiding us moment-by-moment as we meet the 'inner cards' and life's experiences and make choices in relation to them.

We realize the 'inner cards' as another 'layer of personality' often referred to as the 'Lower Self.' I refer to it as the 'Earthly Self nature', for it is what is handed to us this life- time to experience and make choices in relation to.

The Inner Presence[2] is often referred to as the 'Higher-Self.' I refer to it as the 'God-Self nature'.

This Inner Presence has always been within us, but it has become 'lost' to us because we have become caught and 'lost' in:

- Life and its better or worse experiences.
- The pull of the 'inner cards' handed to us.
- Conditioning, or social demands, or patterns either passed to us by our ancestors or self-created for one reason or another (be it as a survival mechanism, or 'to please', or to 'belong', or whatever else).

Sometimes this happens one bit at a time other times it happens with a 'bang'; sometimes it happens consciously and knowingly and other times we hardly notice.

Nevertheless, Inner Presence is never really 'lost' and is constantly trying to make itself heard. It keeps whispering to us in many ways, as when we –

----

[2]There are many terms to define 'Inner Presence' including - Essence, Source Within, God Self Nature, Higher Self – they all refer to the core of our being, the flame of the Life Force that we are. Throughout the text different terms will be used in accordance with what feels to fit best in the context.

- Feel deep compassion for someone, even a total stranger or someone we regard as 'our enemy.'
- Are inspired to act selflessly to help, or protect or cater to the need of another person, an aniomal or nature.
- Hear within with sharp clarity, wise and loving solutions to a dilemma that has been plaguing us, are presented with clear answers to questions we asked, or are offered a deep insight of some kind.
- Are filled with joy, love, hope, or trust.
- Burst with inner freedom and courage knowing that we have the capacity to make choices guided by true love, creativity and wisdom, and overcome conditioned 'right', 'wrong', and 'should' in which we may have been feeling imprisoned.

And much more...

Sometimes we notice, other times we do not; sometimes we listen, mostly we do not; sometimes we act on it, mostly we do not... Sometimes we use these 'Aha' experiences as a catalyst to look within and allow them to grow, but mostly we regard them as a 'one off' moment or a moment of 'unreality' and we jump back to 'our reality'... But we can also choose to be true to this Presence within, listen to it and let it leads and guide us. The more we do so, the more this Inner Presence will expand and strengthen within us and we will begin to experience it as *who we really are* and as *our true Inner Source*.

And the journey further unveils...

We will begin to experience a 'link' between this Presence within and a 'Bigger Presence' of awareness, love, intelligence, creativity, and wisdom, and realize this 'Bigger Presence' as the Greater Source of this Presence within… As a drop in the ocean originates from the ocean, is made of the ocean, contains the ocean within it, and is inseparable from it; as an energy vibration originates from its field of energy, is made of this field of energy, contains the energy field within it, and is inseparable from it; so is the relationship between Inner Presence – our Inner Source - and the 'Bigger Presence' – the Greater Source.

We realize that –

- This Inner Presence that we essentially are is a spark of the 'Bigger Presence', it originates from it and is made of it.
- The nature of Inner Presence - a nature of awareness, love, intelligence, creativity, and wisdom - is a projection of the nature of the 'Bigger Presence' manifesting within each of us in its own beautiful way.
- There is no separation between Inner Presence and the 'Bigger Presence'. We begin to experience the truth that we can always 'rest' within this 'Bigger Presence' and we can endlessly draw upon its resources for nourishment, or strength or guidance - just as a magnet can naturally draw from a magnetic field.

We also see that this relationship applies not only to us but to all other life forms:

- All life forms come from, are made of, are inseparable from, and contain within them this 'Bigger Presence'.
- At the core of all life forms there is an Inner Presence that is a spark of the Bigger Presence.

- The nature of every life form, every species within it and every individual within it, is a projection of the nature of the Bigger Presence – a nature awareness, love, intelligence and creativity and wisdom - manifesting in its own beautiful way.

We therefore realize that all life is an expression of the one Bigger Presence, that there is no separateness but an underlying Oneness and interconnectedness by means of this Bigger Presence, and that this Bigger Presence (however experienced) is what we call 'God' - an archetypal name and image defining the Source of all life.

This is why I refer to Inner Presence that we (and all life) essentially are as the 'God Self nature', for it is a projection of the nature of the Greater Source within us; it is the 'God Within' us and within all that exists.

With this recognition we finally awaken: We remember who we (and all that exists) really are and we remember the Source Within and Without... We begin to hear the magical music of life and see its beauty and mystery... Unity with all life replaces separateness. Reverence, love, and care for ourselves, each other and all life replaces any possible destruction and intolerance.

We are Home...

This is the journey from within-out.

It may sound complex, long and demanding but it is not. It can be our daily experience and reality... Needing only a willingness to breathe, to soften the body, to open the heart and allow the energy to flow, to stay aware and present to moment-by-moment experiences and allow whatever is without to be, and whatever is within to arise... Then, while *Staying still, aware and centred* (this is the key) allow ourselves to experience it fully, let it unveil to us one layer at a time and take us Home, to the truth of our being.

It is through *openness, awareness,* and *stillness* that we will see the truth of *what is really here* and see it for *what it really is* rather than our inner chatter and the meaning, stories and images we attach to it. It is through *openness, awareness,* and *stillness* that the inner layers will unveil, and we will see the truth of *who we really are* - Inner presence - and the truth of the source of this Inner presence that we are - the *Greater Source*... Only when we see these truths will we realize that –

- There is vast array of possibilities available to us and we are totally free to choose.
- When we allow the intelligence, love, creativity, and wisdom that we truly are to lead us, and when we are open to receive the resources of the Greater Source - we have all the resources we need to make choices that are peaceful, joyful, and loving to ourselves, to others and to all life.
- Our choices can be flowing and evolving rather than closed and fixed allowing us to live one day, one moment at a time.

With ongoing *openness, awareness,* and *stillness* we are indeed Home.

Journeying from Without In ...

The Journey from without-In although unfolding from a different direction, results in the same realizations. It is often a response to a curiosity about life, its origin, and our purpose, or to some dilemma that life poses. Sometimes, an 'Aha' experience acts as a magnet that allows curiosity to grow or questions to arise.

Curiosity is innate in us; we all have questions about life and an abundance of 'Aha' experiences pointing to the magic and mystery of life. We often ignore the calling or put it in the 'too hard basket' or judge it to be 'silly'. If we listen and choose to explore – be it from a spiritual perspective or a scientific perspective - we will come to see the wonder of life, the oneness and interconnected-ness of all there is, and realize who we really are as an existence, as humans and as individuals.

The journey from without often begins with the exploration of 'matter' - An exploration that even the great scientific minds of Darwin, Einstein and Hawkins could not fully fathom. When they followed any matter to its origin, they always came to the same realization:

All matter breaks down into organ systems; organ systems break into cells and cells into molecules; molecules break into atoms and atoms into sub-atomic particles... With these sub-atomic particles, the mystery begins because they are elementary and cannot be 'broken down', they do not have a known 'beginning', component or structure and their origin remains a mystery. These sub-atomic particles are energy frequencies of either posi-tive (protons), neutral (neutrons), or negative (electrons) nature and are attracted to each other by a mysterious and unexplained magnetic power. By means of this magnetic attraction they create 102 atoms which are the building blocks of the entire universe and everything within it, including us.

All that exists in the universe - be it our bodies, or a tree, a flower or any animal, a rock, or a grain of sand – is a variation deriving from these 102 atoms. Just as timber taken from the same tree can be shaped into a boat or bowl or table or chair, so it is with us and all that exists: "Everything is made up of the exact same thing, whether it is your hand, the ocean or a star" (John Assaraf, in Rhonda Byrne, 2006, *The Secret*, p. 155).

We realize certain unescapable truths:

1. The Oneness of all there is - for we and all that exists are a 'variation' of the same elementary atoms.
2. The interconnectedness of all matter.

    All life is nourished by the same minerals - The minerals in the earth feed and nourish vegetation and vegetation feeds and nourishes animals and our bodies.

    The same air nourishes all life - We and animals breathe certain elements of the air (oxygen) and release into the air the elements necessary for vegetation (carbon-dioxide) and vice versa.

    The same water circulates and hydrates all life - Ice melts into water and feeds rivers, lakes and oceans; water arises from rivers, lakes and oceans; and returns as rain; rain provides us water, nourishes the earth, and replenishes back the rivers, lakes, and oceans.

    There is a magical and precise eco-system that is the machine of all life and we realize that how we behave within this system not only impacts it, but also impacts us for better or worse.
3. Since these sub-atomic particles are essentially energy frequencies and the 102 Atoms from which all is made are made of these sub-atomic particles - then all that exists is essentially a certain energy frequency! Indeed, if you put your hand under a microscope you will see vibrating

energy. The universe and the physical world of matter are simply condensed energy units.

This enforces the oneness and interconnectedness of all life, and we realize another truth...

4. Energy never vanishes it just changes form. Therefore, all life (including us) – being energy manifesting as matter - cannot and does not vanish but rather changes form, just as water evaporates into steam when heated... In the words of Mary Frye (1932):

Do not stand by my grave and weep,
I am not there, I do not sleep,
I am a thousand winds that blow,
I am the diamond glint of snow,
I am the sun on ripened rain,
I am the gentle autumn rain....

Realizing all these truths gives us a sense of reverence for life in all its forms and takes us deeper...

First, we see that since these sub-atomic particles upon which all life is founded are energy frequencies originating from an unknown source, it is inevitable that this 'unknown source' is the source of all life and that it itself is energy. In other words, we realize that there is one Life Force Energy from which all life emanates.

Paradoxically the world of science which dispels the notion of 'God', has unintentionally discovered that all life is energy orig-inating from and existing by the grace of one field of energy. Scientists are saying what spiritual teachers have been telling us for thousands of years:

"You go to a quantum physicist and you say: What created the World? And he or she will say Energy. Well describe Energy. OK, it cannot be created or destroyed, it always was, always has been, everything that ever existed, always exists, its moving into form, through form and out of form. You go to a theologian and ask the question: What created the Universe? And he or she will say God. OK describe God. Always was and always has been, never can be created or destroyed, all that ever was, always will be, always moving into form, through form and out of form. You see, same description, just a different terminology" (James Ray in Rhonda Byrne, 2006, *The Secret*, p.158).

As his life came to a close, Darwin conceded that his inability to fathom the origin of evolution of these tiny sub-atomic particles and the force that motivates them to move towards evolution, pointed to the existence of something that is more than 'accidental evolution'.

This leads to a second realization.

Whether one believes that this amazing universe arose by mean of 'accidental evolution' or holds to the notion of 'purposeful creation' - the 'conflict' begins to dissipate...

On one hand one realizes that the universe and all life in it, is the greatest 'work of art' and 'scientific invention' and that such tantalizing creation/ invention cannot happen purely by 'accidental and non-purposeful evolution' any more than the Mona Lisa, or the statue of David, or the Taj Mahal, or any great work could happen by 'accidental non-purposeful evolution' - there is a 'force' beyond this universe.

On the other hand, one realizes that no work of art, magnificent creation or invention happens by the wave of a wand but through a process of evolution, of trial and error. Evolution is an inevitable part of the process of creation.

We understand that there can be no 'evolution' without 'creation' or creation' without 'evolution'. Same is with the universe and all life. The conflict between 'creation' and 'evolution' is of our own making. The notion of the scientific Big-Bang is exactly this: an explosion of energy from which all life emanates, and which set in motion (created) the process (the evolution) of life.

Third, we realize that just as it takes awareness, love, intelligence, and creativity to create any work of art or to make great inventions and discoveries, so it is with our universe with its planets and all the life forms on it. It takes immense awareness, intelligence, creativity, love, and passion to bring it all into being. We therefore realize that the Life Force Energy from which all life emanates (this that we call God) cannot be 'blank' but must have/ be infinite awareness itself, it must have/ be infinite intelligence, wisdom, creativity, love, passion, and all other qualities required to manifest the work of art called the universe and life.

Fourth, since all there is, including us, comes from and is made of this Life Force Energy, then all there is (including us) must at essence be this Life Force Energy with its awareness, love, passion, intelligence, and creativity – in the same way that a flame from a fire is the fire and a drop in the ocean is the ocean... More still, just as a drop of the ocean is always connected to its Source – the ocean – and is nourished and replenished by it; just as a spark of the fire is always connected to its Source – the greater flame – and is nourished and replenished by it; so are we and all there is always connected to our Source - the Life Force Energy – and can be nourished and replenished by its infinite awareness, love, intelligence and creativity - all we need to do is be aware of, and in flow with, this connection.

Hence, we begin to remember who we and all there is really are at essence; we realize that life forms differ from each other only by the way awareness, intelligence, creativity, and love manifest through them. For example, while awareness is present in all life forms, in some (i.e. the elements) it is 'dormant, in others (i.e. vegetation) it is subtle, in some (i.e. animals) it is awake but not fully, and yet in others (i.e. humans) it has the potential to be fully awake; likewise, intelligence and creativity are present in all life forms, and love is the nature of all life forms but they manifest in different capabilities and in their own way in each life form, in various species within these life forms and in individuals within these species... We are all essentially the same even as we are different.

Glimpsing the big picture hopefully acts as an incentive to continue the journey and encourages us to look within and become aware of this Essence within us. This Essence is Inner Presence or the God Self nature within, and if we are willing to be still, we will begin to be aware of its voice. The more aware of it we are, the more we recognize that it has always been within us and has always spoken to us, even if in just a whisper, but we did not always listen, or recognize it for what it is: Who we truly are. Once recognized, we can finally choose to bring it to light and allow it to lead the way, and as we do, we will begin to remove the masks.

We will start to see our instinctive drives, innate needs, desires, gifts and challenges, and the vast personal and collective genetic heritage alongside this Inner Presence, and we will begin to recognize them as the 'inner cards' handed to us (the Earthly Self nature).

We will start to see how we have treated these 'inner cards' until now and the choices we have made in relation to them, and that which we call 'Me' (the psychological-self) will begin to unveil and we will see it for what it is - A collection of choices we have made in relation to the 'inner cards' and to life experiences; patterns of expressing, defending, and hiding; beliefs and stories we told ourselves about ourselves, others, life etc or absorbed from our parents, teachers, country, culture etc and took on as truths.

Now, guided by the love, intelligence, and creativity of that which we are at essence - Inner Presence - we can begin to free ourselves... We can own these 'inner cards' with a loving acceptance and make loving and wise choices in relation to them... We realize that we are free to revive old choices or to make new ones, and we are free to review our choices moment-by-moment as we want and as needed.

There is a beautiful new alignment and new wholeness within. We live from inside out and all our choices are guided by our deepest essence - This Inner Presence that we essentially are.

We no longer feel the need nor want to wear a mask for the outside world (the 'Persona').

We feel at one not only with ourselves, but also with others and with all of life for we know we are all One, interconnected and part of the one Source of Life. We begin to hear the magical music and come Home.

Like the journey from within-out, the journey from without-in is not complicated and is subject to the same willingness to breathe, soften the body, open the heart, and stay aware and present to the moment-by-moment experiences, to the questions posed to us by life and to the ongoing gifts of insights, realizations and 'Aha' moments given to us. It requires that instead of 'letting these pass' we use them as a key to set out on a journey of exploration that will take us Home - to the truth of the Oneness of all life, the truth of the nature of all existence and of who we really are as humans and individuals.

Coming Home...

Being human offers us all the potential to complete this journey because we were gifted with the potential for full consciousness, or in the words of Zen: The gift of the potential to be life knowing itself.

Being 'life knowing itself' means we have the potential to realize both the 'inner cards' given to us (the Earthly-self nature), and that which we truly are - this Inner Presence of awareness, love, intelligence, creativity, and wisdom as manifesting within us (God-self nature).

It means that we can know ourselves as Inner Presence and allow the love, wisdom, and creativity we are to lead us and guide us in living, expressing, and making choices in relation to the 'inner cards' and life's experiences. We can be sustained and supported from within.

It means we have the potential to live fully and authentically, be whole with ourselves, with others and with all of life. We can be a vehicle of service and contribution not just to our well-being but to humanity, to all life and to the Life Force Energy itself.

No other life form has this potential.

Fulfilling it and living by it is not only our gift and power but also our human purpose and our responsibility to the Life Force Energy and its flame within us (Inner Presence).

We all have an innate inner pull and longing to fulfil this potential. We also have the free will to follow this inner pull and longing to utilize this potential and live by it, or not.

Many of us fall into the later not because we are 'bad' but because we become caught with the 'inner cards', with our inner experiences and with life experiences, demands and the demands of others.

Sometimes we vaguely remember - maybe something 'keeps gnawing within' us' and we keep longing for something but not knowing what. Other times we ignore, avoid, or even deny the existence of who we truly are – this Inner presence – and its Infinite Source, believe it to be 'unreal', a 'fairy tale' or 'wishful thinking'... unintentionally we deny that by the grace of which we exist. We forget the Oneness and interconnectedness of all life and fall into separateness and aloneness or worse into greed and destruction.

Then we wonder why we feel 'empty', or powerless, or imprisoned; why life seems 'lacking' and why the world and humanity are struggling, and we ask: 'Where is the love, the wisdom, and the freedom?'

We fail to see that we and our world are simply a reflection of this 'forgetting'.

Hopefully, sooner or later we feel compelled to set out on a journey of re-discovery and Home Coming - Home to ourselves and all we are, to the Source within (our Essence – Inner Presence) and without (the Greater Infinite Essence from which we come), to humanity and to all other forms of life... And whether we journey from within or without, because we are all part of the One Source, we can be supported by those who have travelled the path before us although, because are also each a different expression of the Source, we may need to find our own version of the path.

Religion = An Offered Path for coming Home and Staying Home

This is what a 'religion' is – The offering of a path so that we do not forget who we are and find the way Home if/ when we get lost.

Every religion started with someone's realization/ rediscovery of who they are. With someone re-experiencing the Source within them – this Inner Presence of benevolent power, freedom, love, intelligence, and wisdom – and its connection to a Greater Source which is realized to be the Source of all life. It starts with some-one's realization that this Inner Presence is in all life; with experi-encing the Oneness and interconnectedness of all life; and with seeing the beauty, the inherent goodness and moral precept that naturally emanate from all these experienced and realized truths.

Every religion started with an unchangeable commitment made to these realized truths coupled with a calling and a genuine desire to share them with the rest of humanity, to support and guide others to experience and realize them, and to ensure that these truths are neither lost to them nor to humanity. Therefore, an 'established path', or 'a system of practices' of 'how to' was put in place to raise human consciousness, to prevent or minimize the possibility of getting lost, and to offer a way back if lost.

There is nothing bad or evil about this.

As long as humans exist so will religions because the gift of the potential for conscious 'self-knowledge' comes hand in hand with the innate pull and the personal longing for our inner and outer Source – it is our Soul's longing for itself and its Source. Without this pull and longing the potential for conscious 'self-knowledge' cannot materialize. We are like a magnet pulled towards its magnetic field... There is nothing 'weak' or 'primitive' about this innate longing, on the contrary, it calls us to move towards higher consciousness, towards our individual and collective human calling, purpose, and responsibility.

This very same call is the fire that ignited the evolution/ creation of life. It is the call of the Life Force longing for itself - to express, manifest and know itself. It motivated life forms to evolve and grow in awareness until a life form capable of knowing itself and its Source – humanity – arose. It is the same fire that is calling us Home...

When asking those who claim they do not need a 'path' what they believe in and what guides them, the answer is often that they just believe in 'nature' or 'energy' or similar, that they are guided simply by love, or kindness, or justice, or the essential good of humanity and all life etc. Unwittingly, they found their path and the way Home to their inner Source and the Outer Source even as they scoff at religion and deny the existence of the Source within and without. They do not realize that they hear the music but just use a different terminology.

Individuals who may say that they believe in a 'chaotic world', in pure survival or in 'looking after number one' also have a 'path', but it is the noise that they hear rather than the music...

Religion is a human 'prerogative' because no other form of life has been graced with the gift of the potential for conscious self-knowledge and therefore with the conscious/ unconscious longing and pull to know its Soul and its Source... Paradoxically, it is also because other forms of life do not have the gift of the potential for conscious self-knowledge, that they are far less vulnerable to become lost and their path Home is an instinctive offering.

This is at the essence of the mystery of religion... But there are still countless questions and dilemmas regarding religion that await to be answered.

Chapter 2:
There is Nothing New Under the Sun

There seems to be a puzzling contradiction:

On one hand there is the realization that every religion started with –

- Someone's experienced re-discovery of who they and all life really are, of life's interconnectedness and oneness and of the Source of all life.
- A commitment to these experienced re-discoveries.
- A genuine desire to share them with others and to support and guide others "Home."

On the other hand, there is the recognition that today's world is abundant with fine spiritual travellers, seekers, and re-discoverers. Look at the abundance of self-help/ self-development books in bookstores and libraries - books written by many who have trodden the path, who were gifted with insights and realizations to make the same re-discoveries and who genuinely want to share these with the rest of humanity with the intention to support others and bring humanity forward. Writers like Wayne

Dwyer, Louise Hay, Virginia Satire, Gary Zukav, Scott Peck, Katy Byron, Brandon Bays are but a few to mention.

My own book, *"To Life - A Journey of Home Coming and Re-Discovering Our Self and Our Humanity"* and my current writing, are the outcome of the same process of treading the path and receiving the gifts of insights and realizations that I now want to share with others hoping it supports them and contributes to raise human consciousness even if only a little.

While many readers are aided by these writers and some writers even have 'followers', their offerings do not become a 'religion', nor are they intended to.

Therefore, the puzzle:

- What made the discoveries, insights and realizations of past seekers and discoverers like Abraham, or Moses, or Jesus, or Buddha, or Muhammad and so on, different?
- Is there something they offered that today's re-discoverers and teachers do not?
- How is it and why is it that all the major religions practiced today have been established long ago, and that no new major religions have been established today even though wise spiritual teachers abound?

Cynics may be quick to say humans are less gullible today while some critics may say that today people are too intellectually arrogant, too closed and detached from their spiritual core to embrace a new religion. I realized the answer lies in the words 'versions of the same'.

The gifts of insights and realizations regarding the truths about existence and who we and all life are at essence, about life's oneness and inter-connectedness and the Source of all life - were all given to humanity long ago. The great masters of the past have already realized all these truths, they committed to them and shared them hoping to raise human consciousness. Once shared, these truths touched a mass of followers and like a 'tidal wave' the commitment expanded... An 'established system' of practices was put into place to express and embed these realized truths, lest they be forgotten or lost not only to the discoverer and their followers, but to humanity... A religion was born...

All of today's 'discoveries' are a re-discovery and a 'version of' these already realized truths.

In *"To Life – A Journey of Home Coming and Re-Discovering Our Self and Our Humanity"* I stated: "There is really nothing new about my experience and discovery – it was experienced and discovered by many before me and pointed to by spiritual teachers from the beginning of time" (p20). With the gifts of my own experiences and insights I finally realized them to be true and put them together to create a 'path' that sustains me and that I hope will connect with others and support them in their journey Home.

In other words - There is nothing new under the sun...

All the teachings of today's re-discoverers, writers, and teachers are founded on discoveries, insights and realizations already made in the past. Their offerings are the old 're-arranged' and offered in a new variation with the hope that this variation connects with others, support them to become part of the 'tidal wave', create their own variation of it and come Home to their Soul and its Source.

Chapter 3:
Why does Evil Exists?

I f it is true that –

- There is a Oneness and interconnectedness of all life.
- This Oneness is the Greater Source, or God (however perceived)[3] and is essentially good and beautiful benevolent power, freedom, love, intelligence, and wisdom.
- We and all that exists are a flame of this Oneness and therefore are at essence this very same essentially good and beautiful benevolent power, freedom, love, intelligence, and wisdom.

Then -

There must be an inherent beauty, goodness and moral precept emanating from all that exists, and evil cannot and should not exist... But it does...

---

[3]There are various descriptive terms for the Oneness including: Greater Source, God, the God Without, Universe, Greater Essence etc. They all refer to The Source of all life. Throughout the text different terms will be used in accordance with what feels most fitting in the context, but readers are welcome to change it to the descriptive term that connects best with them.

Therefore -

These 'truths' must be but 'wishful thinking'... This Oneness and all that exists including us cannot be essentially good and beautiful, rather, essentially selfish, and corrupt.

This dilemma has led many, especially if they have experienced evil, to give up on the truth of Oneness and its essential beauty and on the truth of the essential beauty of all that exists including themselves... But nothing could be further from the truth... For as Casius told Brutus:

"The Fault dear Brutus is not in our stars but in ourselves, that we are underlings." (Julius Caesar, 1,2, 140-141).

The evil we see is not testimony that these truths are not true - There is an essentially good and beautiful Oneness underlying all life and we humans are part of it... The evil in our world is testimony to human misunderstanding and failing.

The Power and Gift of Full Consciousness and the Free Will to use it

In many ways, we humans are the same as other forms of life, but we differ in one fundamental way: we are the only life form bestowed with the gift of the potential to be fully conscious beings, we have the capacity to see and know all that we are.

This gift comes with tremendous powers: the power of freedom of choice, of free will, of higher intelligence, of being co-creator of ourselves and our world, and of having 'dominion' on other life forms. With these powers come tremendous responsibility.

Whether we use this gift with its potential and power or not, and how we use it, is entirely up to us - for we have the power of free will...

We can choose to use this gift and journey within as described in Chapter 1:

Be willing to see the Persona mask; unveil the mask of the Psychological-self and see it for what it is; go deeper and see the 'inner cards'; and go deeper yet to re-discover that which we essentially are – the Essence of still and aware Inner Presence with its love, intelligence, creativity and wisdom as manifesting within it... Once seen, we can allow this Essence to guide us as we embrace and own the 'inner cards' and the choices we made in relation to them (the 'psychological-self') - we can change patterns, beliefs, and stories if they require changing; we can heal what requires healing; and we can retain what is valuable... Inevitably, we remove the masks...

We can also choose not to journey...

The existence of personal and collective evil is subject to choosing not to journey... That is not to say that everyone who does not journey is evil, rather, it leaves us open and vulnerable to stumbling because... Such a choice enables us to deny, ignore, repress, or identify with the Persona, the Psychological-self and the 'inner cards'; it leaves us vulnerable to being blind to them - and that which we are blind to inevitably owns us and leads us - we are at its mercy and its slave; and depending on the nature of this Persona, Psychological-self and 'inner cards', we can be led astray.

Conscious, or unconscious personal and/ or collective acts of evil are born through the un-willingness to come Home, but they are not the only cause to the existence of evil.

The Full cycle of Dark and light & The Freedom to Choose

We need to understand and realize -

The truth that the Oneness is at essence benevolent power, freedom, love, intelligence, and wisdom – in other words, is essentially good and beautiful; that as a flame of this Oneness, we and all that exists are also at essence benevolent power, freedom, love, intelligence, and wisdom – in other words, essentially good and beautiful...

Does not mean that –

This Oneness, we, and all that exist are devoid of darkness, for indeed, the Oneness, we, and all that exist contain the full spectrum of light and dark...

Light and Dark are like a two-sided coin, the counterparts of a complete cycle that contains the full spectrum. Just as we have day and night, summer and winter, rain and sunshine etc, so too do we have love and hate, courage and cowardice, joy and sorrow, freedom and slavery, kindness, and cruelty etc, and so too do we have good and evil. The full spectrum exists within the Oneness and within all that exists including us...This does not discredit or contradict the existence of the light or the truth that Source and all that exists including us are essentially good and beautiful.

The light is the natural state of being. The dark is what existence - even Inner Presence and the Greater Source - can fall into if not mindful...

When we go within to meet the Essence of who we are, it is the light that meets us... If it is the darkness that first meets us, we must know that the light is still there beneath it and at the core of it. Rather than 'believe' the darkness and choose to follow it; rather than fear it, deny it, ignore it, repress it or struggle with it; we can choose to meet it, accept and own it, bring it to light and be willing to go another layer and allow the light at its core to shine and lead.... Otherwise, just as with the persona, psychological-self, and 'inner cards', the darkness can own us, and we can be at its mercy and its slave.

It is not in the absence (or non-existence) of darkness that the truth of the essential light within us shines, and peace, goodness, and beauty manifest, but rather in the willingness to see and meet the darkness when it arises... Evil arises when we fail to realize this.

Carl Jung, the famous Swiss psychiatrist wisely claimed that one of the purposes of the human gift of full consciousness and free will is so that the Oneness can bring its own darkness into being to shine light on it and integrate it... So, it may be.

The Universe Abides by the Law of Free Will

We also need to realize the truth that the Universe abides by the law of 'free will', otherwise, our 'will' is not 'free'.

We have realized that evil arises when we use the power of our free will to make certain choices:

1. When we choose not to utilize the potential to be fully conscious, and not to journey to rediscover the light of our true essence and let it lead. Instead of embracing and owning the persona, psychological-self, and inner cards, we fear, or deny, or ignore, or struggle with them, and inevitably fall prey to them and become their slave.

2. When we choose not to face, embrace, and own the darkness; when we do not recognize and accept it as part of the cycle of dark and light within us; when we fail to bring it to light and bring light to it. Instead, we either choose to believe it and follow it, or to fear it, deny it, ignore it, struggle with it, and consequently, we fall prey to it, we let it own us and we become its slave.

Whatever we choose, the Universe must say 'yes' to. It will not 'interfere' to stop us or change our choices. It will abide by the gift of free will given to us, and the gift of the power to be co-creator of ourselves and our reality. However, there is a universal law of 'karma' - of consequence (not 'punishment') - and whatever we choose will come back to us and our world sooner or later and in one way or another. It is up to us what shape our reality takes.

Conclusions

When we recognize these truths, we will stop discrediting the light within us and others, within all there is, and within the Source of all there is. We will begin to see that whatever energy we (or our fellow-human) project - an equal energy will be projected back.

We will see that we (and our fellow-human) are fully responsible personally and collectively for what is created in our inner and outer worlds. When we see this, we hopefully choose to use the gifts of free will, of the potential for full consciousness and of the power to be co-creator, wisely and lovingly and a miracle will happen... While it may be inevitable for the darkness to exist, it not only loses power but also begins to transform, for with the light of consciousness shining on it, it can be seen for what it is, and with the power of free will, it can be embraced, owned, and guided wisely and lovingly by the light of the Essence within us and its Source without us... Then, in the darkness of the night we have the light of the moon and the stars to show us the way.

Chapter 4:
One Truth – Why Different Religions?

Equally bewildering as the question of 'good' and 'evil' is the following dilemma:

If it is true that all religions are founded on the truths about the nature of existence, who we are as human beings and individuals, life's Oneness and inter-connectedness, and the one Source of all life - why are there various religions (each with its unchangeable commitment)? And why does each religion claim to be the 'true' path to these truths?

One Destination, yet Many Paths

'Many roads may lead to Rome', likewise, many paths may lead to a shared destination.

All mountain climbers share the ambition to reach the top of the mountain. Every climber recognizes that there are various paths one can take when endeavouring to reach the top. Each climber chooses a path that aligns with their ambition and needs.

The same is true with religion...

All religions share the one destination:

The realization and re-discovery of the truths about the nature of existence and who we are as humans and as individuals, about the Oneness and interconnectedness of all life and the one Source of all life. All religions are committed to these truths and desire to preserve them, bring them in to daily living, share them with others so they too realize and re-discover them, and raise human consciousness. In other words, all religions desire to support Home Coming.

Just as there are various paths one can take to reach a mountain top, there are various religion to reach these truths and come "Home". Every religion offers a different path through which these truths can be realized, preserved, and brought to daily life.

Religions differ because we are all different from each other just as we are the same as each other and while 'discoverers' aimed to realize and re-discover the same truths, they realized them in different ways. Different religions will appeal to different seekers; we are free to appreciate the diversity and choose in accordance with our Soul's calling.

To really grasp the difference between religions we must understand why 'discoverers' realized the same truths in different ways. This requires that we recognize the difference between 'core truths' and 'absolute truths.'

'Core truth' Vs 'Absolute truth'

As we journey to come "Home" we are given the gifts of many insights. Each insight is appropriate and supportive and is offered at the time and in the form that we, the seekers, are ready to receive.

However, an insight is not necessarily a realization. It often is one layer or one stepping-stone that brings us closer to a certain realization. Thus, insight by insight we eventually have an 'Aha-Aha' moment when we experience and know without doubt that the cycle of unfolding layers of insights has completed and a realization of a personal and/or collective nature has been touched. To this realization we are called to make a commitment.

A realization is a realized truth or a core truth.

But a core truth is not necessarily the absolute truth. The absolute truth is often larger and encompasses a kaleidoscope of many core truths.

One may look at the sky on a clear day, see its bright blue colour and realize the core truth that the sky is blue. Another person may look at the sky when it is covered with light clouds and realize it to be blue and white. Someone else may realize it to be grey when seeing it covered with rain clouds. As the sun begins to set the sky is realized to be red and orange. Once the sun is fully set the sky's 'true' colour will be realize as black till the moon and the stars shine – then its 'true' colour is realized to be black with shining lights. The absolute truth about the colour of the sky encompasses the kaleidoscope of all these core truths.

Likewise, it is true with religion.

Within the absolute truths about the nature of existence, of who we are as humans and individuals, of the Oneness underlying all life, and the one Source of all life, there is a kaleidoscope of core truths, and each religion offers a path founded on and adhering to different core truths.

Religions differ from each other in the core truths upon which their paths are founded and to which they adhere because they have been established by different seekers to whom life posed different questions even though they all shared the one desired destination. As these seekers journeyed, it is the core truths answering their questions that made themselves known to them, shone brightly for them, and became central in their journey to the absolute truth. Therefore, to them the seeker made an unchangeable commitment... There is nothing contradictory with that...

The core truths to which a religion adheres and upon which its path is founded act as an entry point from which the absolute truths about the nature of existence, of who we are as humans and individuals, of the Oneness underlying all life, and the one Source of all life, can be reached, and from which the full kaleidoscope of core truths can be unveiled.

Thus, the core truths of love, compassion, mercy, forgiveness etc, to which Christianity adheres and are central to it, form the foundation of its path and act as its entry point to the absolute truths and to the kaleidoscope of core truths. Islam adheres to the core truths of submission, surrender, devotion etc; they are central to it and form the foundation of its path and act as its entry point to the absolute truths; Same is true to Buddhism and its core truths of non-attachment, non-possession, stillness etc and to Judaism and its core truth of Oneness. (paradoxically, Judaism's core truth aligns with the absolute truth. This will be understood in the second part of this book).

If a religion is to remain whole and true it must not become locked in its central core truths. It must retain an openness that leaves room to recognize and encompass within itself the full kaleidoscope of core truths even as some may remain central to it and found its path. It must realize its core truths are a micro-cosmos in the macro-cosmos of absolute truths and the kaleidoscope of core truths encompassed within them... Only then can the full music to be heard.

When a religion (or an individual who follows it), becomes locked within its central core truths and closes the door on other core truths, there is an inevitable fall. First, the religion (or the individual) becomes rigid, disrespectful, destructive, and intolerant to other religions. Second, unwittingly it loses sight of the absolute truths with their beauty, goodness, and moral precept - the very truths that were meant to be reached, preserved, and shared... The music is lost and replaced with noise.

Conclusions

Having various religions is not a 'failure' on the part of religion. It is an expression of the truths that:

- Many roads can lead to the one destination.
- The destination - the absolute truth- encompasses within it a kaleidoscope of core truths and each religion holds at its centre different core truths that act as an entry point to access the absolute truth and its full kaleidoscope.

- We are different as we are the same, even though our journeys share a common destination, the core truths that unveil to us will align with our different orientations, questions and needed lessons.

Failing to recognize this can result in mistakenly discrediting religion and the true shared destination. Worse still, it results with the loss of respect, destructiveness and intolerance between different religions that is so often evident.

The music is lost.

Chapter 5:
The Pitfalls of The 'Package Deal'

One of the most bewildering dilemmas regarding religion comes with the questions:

How and why is it that religion, which aims to support, nourish, and sustain us, elevate us, and ensure that we do not get lost and if we do - show us the way Home, all too often fail us?

Why and how is it that the beautiful music of glimpsed truths with their beauty, goodness, and moral precepts turns into noise or even ecstatic madness and into a tool of destruction and suffering?

Every religion has two components:

- The first is *the core truths* which the seeker realized and to which an unchangeable commitment was made. They are the core truths which answered the seekers' questions and shone brightly for them and therefore, became central in their journey to the absolute truths. The core truths are essentially good by their nature, they are the diamond shining at the core of any religion.

- The second is *the path founded on these core truths*. The path offers a system of practices put in place to bring these core truths and their seen beauty, goodness, and moral precept to daily living and to keep the commitment to them alive. I call this path and its system of practices the *'Package Deal'*, and realizing its potential pitfalls is detrimental to shedding light on the above questions.

Life Enhancing 'Package Deal' Vs Life Inhibiting 'Package Deal' ....

Every mountain climber knows not all paths leading to the mountain top are the same.

Some are short, others long; some are easy, gentle, or straight forward, other are rough, difficult, or complex; some can be dangerous, even fatal.

Some paths may allow and encourage, the climber to enjoy the journey and savour the scenery along the way while others may discourage, even prohibit, the climber from enjoying the journey and demand total focus on the destination.

It is up to each mountain climber to choose their path.

A climber may suggest a route to other climbers or may try to convince them to take a particular route; a climber may warn another climber of the dangers of a certain route and offer a 'safer' one, or may point that while the destination is one's vision, the journey is vital too. However, no climber has the right to enforce or impose their suggestion or warning on another. Each climber must choose and bear the consequences for their choice.

Likewise, with any 'package deal' put in place to bring certain core truths to daily living and keep the commitment to them alive.

Every seeker knows, not all 'package deals' are the same, even though they all attempt to express and preserve beautiful core truths and lead to the shared absolute truths.

Some may be gentle, taking seekers by the hand one step at a time while others may be rough and attempt to 'push' the seeker.

Some may be open, they may allow and even encourage the seeker to enjoy the journey of life with its 'scenery', gifts, and opportunities – they are life enhancing; other may be closed and limiting, they may not allow or even forbid the seeker from enjoying the journey of life and experiencing the joy of the 'scenery' – they are life inhibiting and may be all consuming, dangerous, or even fatal.

It is up to each seeker to choose wisely.

A 'package deal' will most likely fail us when it is life inhibiting, all consuming, or worse - dangerous or fatal. It will inevitably fall out of alignment with the core truths it desires to express and protect and be intolerant towards other 'package deals'; it will turn off the music and leave us with the noise.

A seeker may point out to another the benefits or the dangers of a particular 'package deal' and may call attention to the fact that even the highest destination does not justify all means. However, no seeker has the right to enforce or impose a suggestion or a warning on another. Each seeker must choose, and ultimately bear the consequences of their choices. We are each free to choose and responsible for our choices.

Attempting to 'save' someone from a life inhibiting or dangerous 'package deal' forcibly, while understandable, is destructive. Fine balance is needed and while not easy to apply, it is the only respectful and peaceful way.

We cannot blame a religion for its 'package deal', we are the creator of the 'package deal', we choose how to live and preserve realized truths. Recognizing this brings to light another failing.

Unchanged Commitment to Core Truths Vs Their Expressions (the 'package deal')

There is an ongoing danger of failing to distinguish the unchanged commitment made to certain realized truths[4] (or core truths) from the system of practices – the 'package deal' - put in place to bring these truths to daily living and keep the commitment to them alive.

Due to such failing a religion can be incorrectly perceived, judged, and rejected for its 'package deal' rather than its core truths. Worse still, followers of the religion can mistakenly –

1. Shift their focus from the core truths to the 'package deal' and the core truths become lost.
2. Allow the 'package deal' to become 'engraved on stone tablets' and "when circumstances change and a call for a different expression of the same commitment arises – we meet the wall of the engraved do and don't... morality turns

---

[4]Realized truths are Core truths. These terms may be used alternatively throughout the text, but they mean the same.

into moralism..." (*The Mystical Core of Organized religion*, Steindl-Rast David, New Realities, VolX No 4, March-April 1990, pp 35-37).

3. Fail to see that we are different as we are the same. We may share an unchangeable commitment to the same core truths, but we have varied ways to express this commitment. Engraved 'do's and 'don'ts' do not leave room for the varied tapestry of expressions.

Hence, rigid laws replace realized truths. Instead of acting as means of living and preserving the realized truths, these laws become the purpose and the realized truths with their beauty, goodness and moral precepts become lost in rigid adherence to practices. Rigid adherence to practices will inevitably result in blindness and intolerance.

God's writing is not and cannot be engraved, it is rather a freedom of expression to a commitment to certain realized truths, and it is these truths and the commitment to them that is, and must be, the true writing not the chosen expression.

That is not to say that it is not useful, helpful, or even necessary to some extent to have a 'package deal' offering 'ways of doing', 'symbolic acts' and 'Traditions'. They indicate what it means to live the realized truths and how to preserve them and keep the commitment to them alive. They can also act as a path back to the realized truths if they have become lost to us.

However –

* It is always the realized truths that are the real 'diamond' within the 'package deal.' The 'package deal' is just a

collection of 'how to', a means of living and preserving the 'diamond', not a purpose to itself.
- The 'package deal' is an offering of 'guidelines' to support us. While the realized truths and the commitment to them may be unchangeable, the 'package deal' of guidelines is not!
- The 'package deal' with its 'guidelines' must always be aligned with the core truths and the absolute truths and it must always be seen in the context of the place and time it was offered and the language and terminology of that time and place.

If a discoverer and their followers want to keep the fire of the unchangeable commitment to their realized truths burning, they must differentiate it from the 'subscribed expression' = the 'package deal'. Only such separation will allow for ongoing 'freedom of expression' and only ongoing 'freedom of expression' will provide the air needed to re-kindle the fire and keep it alive.

When the door of free expression closes, expression becomes engraved in stone and takes precedence over the realized truths. The airflow is cut, and the fire suffocates...

Brother Steindl-Rast David likened it to stream of lava that flows down the sides of the mountain and begins to cool off: "the farther it got from its origins the less it looked like fire and turned into rock – dogmatism, moralism, ritualism – are layers of ash deposits and volcanic rocks that separate us from the fiery magma deep below." (*The Mystical Core of Organized religion*, New Realities, VolX No 4, March-April 1990, pp 35-37).

Followers, or even 'discoverers', who fail to realize all this, may attempt to keep the fire of an unchangeable commitment to their realized truths alive by closing the door of the 'package deal' rather than leaving it open. The 'package deal' becomes fixed rather than be flexible, and the 'lava grows colder'.

Then, they mistakenly believe that the only way to re-kindle the fire and restore the commitment to the realized truths is by locking the door even tighter – by increasing strictness and rigidity of expression. Unwittingly, the 'lava grows even colder' and the door is further tightened and so on it goes... The 'package deal' and its guidelines become more and more rigid, they take precedence over the realized truths and the unchangeable commitment to them and what one intended to express, live by, and keep alive – the realized truths - slowly fades, and becomes lost... The 'package deal' is bound to fail us and become a vehicle of destructiveness, intolerance and even suffering.

Some may dare to break open the door and give room to new expressions, allow the air to flow and re-kindle the fire of the truths that were realized and the unchangeable commitment made to them. They create a new 'package deal' within the old one – like a path within a path – and others who seek similar new expressions may join them... But this new 'package deal', this path within the path, must stay open lest it too becomes nothing but a new 'closed' personal or collective variation just like the original 'closed established path' they attempted to open... Often the lessons are not learned, and these variations tend to fall prey to the same pitfall. They too may become tightly bonded with their new-found expression - the new 'package deal' - and slowly close the doors on it... And once more, the fire slowly fades.

How wonderful will it be if only we would realize that under the umbrella of any central 'package deal' there can be as many personal variations as there are 'followers'... The fire will never die, it will keep burning in its kaleidoscope of expressions and the music will never become a 'noise'.

Conclusion

The failures explored in this chapter are stumbling blocks to which all religions and all followers are vulnerable.

It is true that some prescribed 'package deals' may be life inhibiting, or even dangerous. However, it is also true that we are the 'creators' of the 'package deals' and that we are free to choose for ourselves how to live and commit to certain realized truths we hold dear. Rather than blame religion, or any 'package deal' offered by any religion, we can take responsibility for ourselves and our choices.

It is true that any 'package deal' can become 'lifeless routines', endless 'mindless repetitions' and engagement in practices just because 'it is how it has always been done', instead of evolving in accordance with the needs and growth of life, of human consciousness and individual calls, so that the deep values can be translated to modern day practices and add value and growth of consciousness into everyday living. However, it is also true that it is not any religion itself, nor any 'package deal' that are at fault or fail us - it is we who are at fault with our misunderstanding and blindness.

It is we who lose sight of the realized truths and absolute truths with their beauty, goodness, and moral precept, lose sight of our commitment to them, and cause the fire to lose its light.

It is we who allow intolerance, destruction, and suffering to be inflicted from one religion on another, from one collective variation within a religion on another, and still from one individual variation on another.

It is we who turn the beautiful music into a loud, even mad, noise.

Chapter 6:
Offering Vs Imposing

The failure to distinguish 'offering' from 'imposing' has been pointed to in chapters 4 & 5. However, since its contribution to the 'noise that drowns the music' is significant, it must be specifically addressed.

The gift of realized truths gives rise to loving these truths, committing to them, and wanting to share them and offer them to humanity. This commitment prompts 'discoverers' and their followers to create a 'path' offering a 'package deal' of prescribed practices to bring these realized truths to everyday living, preserve them and keep the commitment to them alive.

Discoverers and followers must be mindful not to allow this love, commitment, and the desire to share, express and preserve, result in 'imposing' their realized truth or prescribed 'package deal' rather than 'offering' it.

Whenever we fail to see that –

- There are many religions leading to the one destination.
- Any religion and any prescribed 'package deal' even if different to our own, can be just as safe and beautiful and

can offer the traveller the experiences and expressions aligned with their spirit, needs, and calling.
- If a prescribed 'package deal' is 'dangerous', while we can point out this danger, we must not attempt to 'save' a 'traveller' - each traveller is ultimately free to choose and must bear the consequences for their choices...

We are bound to become judgemental, righteous, and attempt to impose on others the religion and the 'package deal' that aligns with us.

Whenever we fail to distinguish 'core truths[5]' from the 'absolute truth' and recognize that –

- The 'absolute truth' encompasses a kaleidoscope of 'core truths'.
- Each religion is founded on and is committed to certain core truths which act as an entry point to the absolute truth and its kaleidoscope of core truths, and each religion must remain open to embrace this kaleidoscope.

We are bound to become locked in righteousness and attempt to impose our path on others.

Whenever we fail to distinguish the realized truths and the commitment to them, from the 'package deal' put in place to express these truths and commitment, and we –

- Become bonded with the 'package deal' rather than the realized truths and our commitment to them.

---

[5] Core truths are the 'Realized truths.' Both terms may be used in this and following chapters, but they mean the same.

- Fail to recognize we are all as different as we are the same and while we may share a commitment to the same realized truths, we may have varied ways of expressing them and committing to them.

We are bound to become rigid, condemn expressions that differ from ours, and attempt to impose our version on others.

It is due to these failing that –

- Islam may reject Judaism and Christianity; Christianity may reject Islam and Judaism. Judaism may reject Buddhism and Christianity; etc.
- Catholic, Anglican, Protestant etc may attempt to impose their variation of Christianity on each other; Shiite and Sunni Muslims may attempt to impose their variation of Islam on each other; Orthodox, Secular, Traditional, Reform etc Jews may attempt to impose their variation of Judaism on each other; etc.
- Individuals within these variations may attempt to impose on each other their individual variations of the variation.

Every religion and its followers, even Atheism, is vulnerable to these failings.

Offering a religion with its core truths to another with a sincere desire to share one's discoveries and realized truths and offer another a way Home is a beautiful gesture. Imposing on another is not. Likewise, offering a 'package deal' to another or pointing out dangers and pitfalls of a certain 'package deal' to another, may express a sincere caring for the other. Imposing on another does not.

No religion has the right to impose itself on another; no 'package deal' has the right to impose itself on another; no variation within a 'package deal' has the right to impose itself on another.

Imposing suffocates the tapestry of expression; it turns off the light of the realized truths with their beauty, goodness, and moral precept; it renders the commitment blind; it drowns out the music and creates an unbearable noise that is rejected, but unfortunately, the beautiful music is rejected with it.

Chapter 7:
In Conclusion...

The previous chapters have hopefully demystified religion and clarified some of the dilemmas in 'the case against religion'.

There is nothing mysterious, complicated, or 'evil' about religion. It is a natural expression of the gift given to us as humans – the gift of the potential to be 'life knowing itself' - and of the innate pull and longing to fulfill this potential, to come Home to realize –

- The nature of existence and who we are as humans and as individuals.
- The divine essence within us and within all that exists and recognize this essence to be who we and all that exists truly are.
- We and all life are sparks of the same Source - the same Life Force Energy.
- The unity and Oneness beneath the external differentiation and variation of expression.

Religion is, because "we are not human beings learning to be spiritual, we are spiritual beings learning to be human" (Jacqueline Small in *Growing Whole*, by Molly Young Brown, 1993, Hazelden

Books). It is, because "our Spirituality is a oneness and interconnectedness with all that lives and breathes, even with all that does not live or breathe" (Mudrooroo).

We have recognized that every religion begins with someone's Home Coming as they realize some of the core truths within the absolute truths about existence, humanity, and the Source of life, and as they commit to these truths and share them with others wanting to support their Home Coming and edge humanity in a new and elevated direction.

Once shared, many were touched and followed.

With sincere intention and a desire to ensure these truths are neither lost to them, nor to the followers or to humanity, a prescribed 'package deal' indicating how to live and preserve these realized core truths was put in place.

Yet, however sincere the commitment and desire, 'discoverer' and followers must be aware to –

- Realize that various religions can lead to the same destination.
- Distinguish 'core truth' from 'absolute truth'.
- Distinguish their 'unchanged commitment' to their realized core truths and absolute truths from its 'expression' (the 'package deal') and be sure they bond with the realized core truths and absolute truth, not with the expression.
- Distinguish 'offering' from 'imposing'.

Otherwise, religion will fail us both individually and collectively. Instead of taking us Home, keeping us Home and pointing the way if we are lost – it will lead us further astray.

Instead of raising us up, moving us forward and sustaining us - it will become a closed and rigid institution and a vehicle for oppression, suffering, destructiveness, and intolerance.

Instead of sustaining the fire of the truths - it will become a vehicle that extinguishes the fire.

The sweet music becomes noise, and the delicate dance becomes ecstatic madness....

But truth is that it is not religion itself who has failed us - we have failed it and ourselves through blindness and ignorance.

Chapter 8:
The Next Step...

It is time for each of us to honestly look within and without and ponder the religion (with its core truths and 'package deal') that we have come to 'just accept', or to eagerly practice, or reject.

It is a journey well worth taking because:

- Regardless of whether we choose to stay faithful to or let go off a certain religion, we will see clearly 'the meeting place' - the thread that connects all religions and all core truths. We will have a clear realization that each religion with its core truths has a place, a purpose, and a contribution to make in the journey to the absolute truths. There is no place for 'separateness', fear, or 'imposing' only openness and appreciation.
- It will result in self re-discovery and personal freedom as with clarity and wisdom we will find the path of our calling to come Home, and with love, tolerance, respect and appreciation for self and others.

The journey begins with the simple question "what is my religion?"

The question of our religion arises often, maybe when we complete certain forms or documents that require information about 'our religion', or maybe through daily conversation. We are quick to name the religion into which we were born, or which was passed to us, or which we chose/'converted' to etc: I am Jewish, Christian, Muslim, Buddhist or 'I am an Atheist', a non-believer, and so on.

This only addresses the fact that by birth or otherwise, we are part of a 'particular family' - be it the Jewish family, or the Christian family, or the family of Islam etc.

However, here it is a different kind of questioning that we need to ask ourselves. For whether we are 'believers' or 'non-believers', whether we practice the religion of our birth or have rejected it to choose another or none, the questions here are:

How have I reached this position?
Did I just accept it as a matter of fact?
Did I decide on basis of what was passed on to me in 'Sunday School' or on basis of my experience (whether positive or negative)?

If we are to honestly answer to the question of 'What is my religion?' and decide whether we believe, or not in a particular religion (or non-religion) and whether we want to be part of it or not, we must be willing to explore deeply and honestly.

The first step requires us to bring to light the story of the religion in question because every religion, even Atheism, has a story with two components:

- One is of a personal nature – the story of the 'traveller' their quest, their journey to the absolute truths through specific realized core truths and their unchangeable commitment to these truths.

For example, Buddha was distressed by the poverty and suffering he saw around him and the richness yet emptiness of his personal life, and he set out to reveal the cause of suffering and 'abolish' it; Jesus was distressed as he watched his land and people conquered by a mighty Empire and witnessed the despair, loss of spirit, hope, love and compassion in the people – a spirit, love and compassion whose fire he wanted to revive; Muhammad was seeking answers for pain in his own life and for the chaotic tribal life of his people; Atheism has been moved by existential questions and by the distress and disenchantment caused by the 'noise' that has replaced the music and the destruction and suffering inflicted by followers of various religions upon each other; etc...

- The other is the collective component - the evolution of the personal story with its realized truths and the commitment to them, as it transformed into a collective path with its underlying message and its 'package deal'.

We must therefore ask ourselves:

Do I *really* know the personal and collective story of the religion into which I was born or which I chose to either reject or practice?

Do I *really* know the nature of its realized truth(s) and unchangeable commitment made to them?

Once the story with its realized truths and commitment is revealed, we need to ask:

Do I *really* want to be part of this story? Why?

Do I *really* want to make a commitment to the truths/messages beyond this story? Why?

It is important to know the 'why' for it reveals our true intentions and whether we really feel aligned with this story, its messages, realized truths and commitment.

If we do feel aligned with a particular story it is time to ask:

How does this religion 'behave' in relation to other religions with their core truths and 'package deals'? Is it disrespectful, intolerant, imposing?

And -

How is this religion in relation to its 'package deal' - Does the 'package deal' really support the living of the realized truths to which a commitment was done? Is the 'package deal' life enhancing or inhibiting? Is it rigid or open? Does it keep the realized truths and the commitment alive or suffocate it? Have the truths become 'lost' in the 'package deal'?

And -

How am I in relation to this 'package deal' - Do I *really* know it? Am I aligned with its expressions of the realized truths and the commitment to them?

Each of these steps requires us to follow Brother David Steindl-Rast's advice and turn our faithfulness or rejection into betrayal, then betrayal into faith, then be part of our chosen truth. We must not be afraid to be open, truthful, and honest in this process. It is helpful to bear in mind the following:

- Faith and betrayal are not about right or wrong, good or bad, but rather an expression of the calling of one's Soul - a realization whether a certain religion with its core truths and 'package deal' is or is not one's calling, and what one is here to live and contribute towards.

- It is mistaken to believe that we must stay with or contribute to the religion into which we were born. Whether we believe our birth into a particular religion to be 'accidental' or 'purposeful' what is important is the willingness to explore, to be still with our deepest self and with the voice of Inner Presence, to be open to the answers – we will be guided...
- An expression of 'faith' does not ask for 'blind faith'. It does not ask that we see the religion with its story, core truths and 'package deal' as faultless. The story of every religion holds both truth and 'myths', and every religion and its 'package deal' will have aspects that invite reviewing, and dirty water to dispose of.

Judaism is the religion into which I was born and within which I grew. It is the religion I felt the need to betray, then either reconcile with or leave behind, and either way regain my own faith and truth. Therefore, the journey of exploration will be directed towards Judaism and Judaism will be the focus of the second part of this book. This does not exclude anyone regardless of the religion they want to explore, as the stepping-stones and insights will support all journeys.

Part 2:

Judaism From A Different Perspective

It is a tree of life for those who grasp it,
And all who uphold it are blessed.
Its ways are pleasantness, and all its paths are peace.

(Wolfson, Marx, 12)

Chapter 9:
The Story of Judaism and its Underlying Message...

Do I *really* know the personal and collective story of Judaism?

Do I *really* know the realized truths upon which Judaism is founded and its unchangeable commitment?

When I explored my Family-Tree I found Judaism well rooted back through many generations, as far back as I could track. Judaism is the family into which I was born and therefore I naturally responded to the question of religion by saying: 'I am Jewish', just as one born into Christianity, or Islam, or Buddhism or other would respond with: 'I am Christian' or 'I am Muslim' and so on.

Judaism, the story of its evolution and the nature of its unchangeable commitment intrigued me from a young age but my relationship with Judaism was conflicted:

I felt a deep and strong connection with Judaism and an appreciation, wonder, and curiosity. Judaism was clearly the path with which my soul connected.

However, I also felt a sense of unease with Judaism. I was unable to reconcile myself with many of the practices and biblical interpretations that were passed on to me as a child.

Allowing for the circumstances of the time and place of my birth, this confusion was hardly surprising ...

I was born in Israel in 1950. The country was barely two years old. There was a sense of chaos and confusion with people pouring in from all four corners of the world, people who apart from the fact that they were all Jewish seemed to have little, if anything, in common.

There were the Jews already living in Israel. They were the Jews who had managed to survive the many exiles imposed on Jews over thousands of years, or who had managed to return following their exile. They carried a 'Palestinian passport' courtesy of the British. Israel had been re-named Palestine – a name imposed on the Jewish people by the Roman conquerors and all the following conquerors of the land of Israel. They were strong Jews with a culture of survival and resistance; a People struggling to keep the Jewish dream of returning "Home" in the face of one conqueror after another and also a growing Arab population slowly trickling in from the surrounding Arab States; a People often at odds with what they perceived as a generally passive/ submissive culture, or an assimilative culture of their exiled brothers and sisters scattered around the world.

There were the Jews who arrived in Israel from Russia before and after the Second World War. As religion was banned in Russia, most knew little, if anything, about Judaism apart from the fact that they were Jewish. They came either because they needed a safe home or had a passion to make real the dream of socialism in the land of Zion.

Following the UN declaration of the State of Israel in 1948, survivors of the Holocaust arrived from various parts of Europe - Germany, Austria, Bulgaria, Poland, Hungary, what was then Czechoslovakia, Belgium, Holland, etc. A 'collection' of Jews with different languages, cultures, foods, and customs. Some were broken in body and spirit and wanted nothing to do with their 'Jewishness' or with God - they came because they had nowhere else to go. Others were immensely grateful for the miracle of their survival they kissed the ground of their new home as they landed and were full of hopes and a commitment to the dream of a renewed Jewish State.

There were those, like my own parents, who came from Africa and the Middle East - Egypt, Iraq, Yemen, Iran, Syria, Morocco, etc. They had not experienced the horrors of the Holocaust and most had lived in reasonable comfort and were loyal contributing citizens in their respective Arab States for many generations. With the UN establishment of the Jewish State of Israel, the Arab States where they were citizens declared them enemies and expelled them. Their contributions and loyal citizenship no longer mattered, they were not wanted, and it was no longer safe to stay. These African and the Middle Eastern Jews not only looked and were different from their 'Palestinian', Russian, and European born brothers and sisters, they also looked and were different from each other – they were a mixture of people with different languages, cultures, foods, and customs. Like their European brothers and sisters, some came full of hope and a vision to fulfil a dream to be part of a Jewish State, while others came broken from all they were forced to leave behind, and some came because they had nowhere else to go.

There was also the internal division between Ashkenazi Jews and Sepharadi Jews - each with their different culture, foods and traditions, even different styles of synagogues and prayers - and between 'orthodox' Jews and 'secular' Jews.

Each of these groups were not only puzzled by the other but often looked down on each other. Each believed themselves to be the more 'civilized' or 'cultured', or 'better Jew' than the other.

All this was confusing enough for the adults struggling to rebuild their broken lives, let alone for young people like myself. There was frustration and heartbreak on one hand and hopes, dreams and enthusiasm on the other. People often argued with each other on buses, at bus-stops, shops, synagogues or wherever they could – arguments that would escalate until someone wise said: 'Stop arguing, it really does not matter, we are all Jews.' Everyone would calm down, smile nervously, shake hands, apologize, and try to explain the source of their despair and pain, or frustration and disillusionment, or hope and gratefulness.

The question left hanging was: Well yes, we are all Jews, but what does it mean to be Jewish beyond the fact that we all happened to be born into this 'Jewish Family'? What is the story of Judaism? What unites us despite our differences?

The Old Testament

We must begin with the Old Testament - the core foundation of Judaism. Within its pages the story, evolution, and purpose of Judaism and the Jewish People is encapsulated. It binds together all Jews wherever they come from and whether they are Sepharadi or Ashkenazi, Orthodox or Secular or Reform - all Jews hold some reverence for the Old Testament.

Not only Jews revere the Old Testament but also Christians and Muslims whose 'stories' are interconnected with Judaism and lay-persons such as historians, archaeologists, psychologists and even scientists. This is not surprising because the Old Testament is a mysterious blend of history and myth, of science and theology/spirituality, of psychology, philosophy and sociology, of law and social justice, even medicine and poetry; all conveying general messages about life, about being human, our place on the planet, our potential strengths and weaknesses, and specific messages about Judaism and the Jewish People. However, while many show some curiosity and reverence to the Old Testament, it is only the Jewish People for whom it holds a central and revered point of reference.

The first five - and most revered - books of the Old Testament are known as the Torah. Within the pages of the Torah the story of Judaism and the Jewish People unfolds. The Torah begins with the story of the world and humanity before focusing on the 'birth' of the Jewish People and becoming a nation. It concludes with Moses' passing.

It is generally held that these first five books - The Torah - were written by Moses himself 'under instructions from God'. While intellectually we may scoff at such a notion, every religion (as we now know) has been founded on someone's reconnection with the Essence within them and realizing this Essence to be a flame of a Greater Essence. If Moses wrote these books, he wrote them from his Essence which is a flame of the Greater Essence - hence, 'under instructions from God'. It is just a matter of language and terminology used in accordance with the time. There is a growing recognition that the Torah was not written by Moses alone, that parts were written by other writers - mostly the Priests (the Kohanim and Levites) of the time, but also other scribes. This may be true and can explain the many puzzling contradictions in the told events, stories, and even in Moses' given commandments and the perception of God, in the Torah and throughout the Old Testament.

The remaining books of the Old Testament – The Prophets and the Holy Writings - continue the story of the People of Israel. They begin with the Israelites entering the land of Canaan led by Joshua after the death of Moses, their settlement on the land, the period of Judges, Prophets and Kings and the evolution of the kingdoms of Israel and Judea until the collapse of the 1st Temple. They also contain a few later periods 'approved to be included' writings. It is a history filled with victories, achievements and failures, ups and downs, losing the path and coming back.

These books are believed to have been written by different writers including the Judges, Kings, Prophets, and Priests of Biblical time and possibly other scribes who added to the texts at later periods.

It is believed that all the stories of the Old Testament, including the Torah, were collated and put together by The Great Assembly (an assembly of 120 scribes, sages, and prophets from the end of the Biblical period to early Hellenistic period) in accordance with writings left behind and found. The Great Assembly may also have played a part in 'editing' the writings.

One must bear in mind that prior to 'writing', personal and collective history and stories were passed down from one generation to the next both orally and by mean of drawing. In her book 'Infidel', the author, Ayaan Hirsi Ali, describes how as a child she had to recite over and over the genesis of her family as far back as was possible. This is exactly how information and stories were passed from one generation to another, and when writers collated recorded stories and put them into writing they would have most likely 'change' details' to –

- Create a complete and flowing story (therefore, in every story of the past there will be a component of truth and a component of myth or fiction).
- Empower some messages using a particular language and terminology (and it is these messages, rather than the 'story' itself, that are important).

The same applies to whoever collated the stories of the Old Testament including the Torah and put them into writings. The writers would have 'edited' (make some 'changes' to the stories, add or subtract from them) to 'fill gaps' or to create a flowing story - therefore, the stories will carry elements of both fact and fiction. They would also have used specific language and terminology to empower certain messages and realized truths about life and humanity in general and Judaism and the Jewish People in particular - and it is these messages rather than the stories as such that matters and are the focus of this book.

Recognizing this we can explore the story of Judaism and the Jewish People – its 'founder', its messages, realized truths and unchangeable commitment.

The story of Judaism, its Core truths, and its Unchangeable Commitment

It is traditionally held that the story of Judaism and the Jewish People began with Abraham. However, 'Judaism' existed well before Abraham. Its story began and evolved from 'the beginning of time' and its founding core messages are encapsulated within the very first chapters of Genesis.

The Oneness

The very first sentence in Genesis states: "In the beginning God created the heaven and the earth" (Genesis 1, 1) – This sentence expresses Judaism's core message that all life is One and all life originates from one Source.

Judaism's central prayer and meditation: "Hear O Israel, the Lord thy God[6], the Lord is One", affirms both recognition of and reverence to the Oneness of all life and to the One Source from which all life, including us, emanates[7]. Without this message of Oneness of Source and life there is no Judaism - A truth recognized and acknowledged well before Abraham.

The Power of The Word

The continuation of the above sentence states: "And God said let there be light and there was light" (Genesis 1, 2) is much more

---

[6]God stands for the Source of Life however one perceives and experiences this Source. What matters here is the recognition and realization that all life originates from one Source however this Source is perceived.

[7]'Emanates' is not a statement of 'creation' or 'evolution' but realizing that all that exists 'heaven' and 'earth' originates from the One Source... If one holds aversion to either notions, it is well to be reminded that in every evolution there is a process of creation and in every creation there is a process of evolution - there is no contradiction between these notions except of our own making...

than an expression of 'magic creation'. It recognizes and respects the power of the Word – A recognition and respect well rooted in Judaism.

Judaism recognizes the saying 'sticks and stones can break my bones, but words can never hurt me' is only applicable once one has recognized the creative and the destructive power that 'Words' can have.

Words matter. They are powerful, meaningful, and can create or destroy. There is much truth in the saying: "Life and Death are in the hands of words" for the greatest of human creation and human destruction, and the deepest human scars begin with the energy given to words...

Today's modern Psychology and teachers – be it Wayne Dwyer, Louise Hays, Rhonda Byrne with 'The Secret', Richard Bandler & John Grim (Founders of NLP - Nero linguistics) and many more - all recognize this and acknowledge the power words have both on a personal and a collective level.

Words are energy that like an arrow are shot to their target and like a boomerang find their way back to the sender... Only when we acknowledge the power of the words, can we use our words effectively and wisely, and 'protect' ourselves from the words of others.

Jewish education invites one to be mindful with the language they use and the words they empower. It also encourages open debate, analysis, and the study of 'words.'

The power of the word is a core truth within Judaism acknowlededged well before Abraham.

The Essential Goodness, Sanctification and Reverence of all Life

Adherence to the essential goodness of life, the sanctification and reverence for all life, are also core truths of Judaism. They arise from the truth of Oneness and were acknowledged before Abram. This is evident in the sanctification: "And God saw that it was good" (Genesis 1;10/12/13/14), that concludes each day of creation/ evolution.

Man's position On the Planet

Judaism recognizes that humans hold a central and domi-nant position on this planet: "And God blessed them and God said to them, be fruitful and multiply, replenish the earth and subdue it: and have dominion over the fish of the sea, and over the birds of the air, and over every living thing that moves on the earth. Behold, I have given you every herb bearing seed, which is upon the face of all the earth, and every tree, on which is the fruit yielding seed; to you it shall be for food" (Genesis 1:28/29).

The underlying messages are clear and portray the core truths of benevolent dominion and ethical eating. (Both will be explored at depth in later chapters). Like many other core truths upon which Judaism is founded, these too were real-ized and expressed well before Abraham and the beginning of Judaism.

The Shabbat

The Shabbat is one of the central practices of Judaism.

The sanctification of Shabbat is articulated in Genesis (2;1-3), well before Abraham and the Jewish People:

"And by the seventh day God ended his work which he had done; and he rested on the seventh day from all his work which he has done; And God blessed the seventh day and sanctified it."

Like all the stories in the Old Testament, the Shabbat needs to be seen for its messages and what they signify rather than for its story.

First, it tells us about life and how it came to be.

The universe did not magically appear in six days. Each day signifies a phase in the process of creation and evolution as life moves from the simple (the elements) to the more complex (various animal life) and finally to the most complex (humanity). This message is relevant not only to life in general but also to our personal life - for it too is an ongoing process of creation and evolution, phase by phase, each taking its time as we move from the simple to the complex be it biologically or psychologically/ spiritually (infancy-childhood -adulthood-old age).

Second, the Shabbat tells us about wise living.

While 'doing' (creation/evolution) is wonderful, we must not get so caught up in it that we forget about 'being' because we will become lost, disconnected, and lose meaning. Stopping the 'doing' and allocating time for 'being' - being still, quiet, and listening – allows us to:

- Re-connect with the Inner Soul, that which we are and with its Source.
- Reflect on the 'doing' – Relax, enjoy, express gratitude, and appreciate the 'doing' with both its achievements and its challenges.

The story of the Garden of Eden

The story of the Garden of Eden reflects the core truths of Judaism about life, its Source, and humanity, and the wisdom of living. It is another testimony to the existence of Judaism well before Abraham was born and before the story of the Jewish People began.

As with the Shabbat, it is important to listen to the story's messages rather than the story itself. When taken metaphorically rather than literally, the story of the Garden of Eden is a wise and beautiful story with everything we need to know about life and living, about what it means to be human, and about human potential strengths and potential downfalls.

The garden of Eden is not a literal garden, it is a metaphor for the planet on which we live - our physical home.

Adam and Eve are not literally the first humans but symbolic representations, for the genesis of humanity clearly begins well before Adam and Eve.

Adam and Eve take the genesis of Abram's Family Tree as far back as was known to the writer and consequently, they act as a metaphor for 'the beginning'. What matters is not the anthropological accuracy but rather the messages of truths about life, living and being human and the consequences of forgetting these truths.

The Tree of Life and the Tree of Knowledge of Good and Evil are not actual physical trees; they too are symbolic representations.

The Tree of Life is a symbol for -

- The Life Force - the Source from which all life emanates (the Source Without), and its flame within everything and everyone including ourselves (the Source Within).
- The nature of life both without us and within us.
- Life and its experiences.

We are advised to 'eat freely' from the Tree of life, meaning to always -

- Stay connected to and in flow with who we are at essence – the flame of the Source within us; and stay connected to the Source of this flame - the Source Without.
- Respect and embrace the nature of life as it manifests within us and within all other life forms.
- Embrace life with its experiences.

The Tree of Judgement of Good and Evil symbolizes the potential gifts and challenges of humans – The gifts of conscious awareness and the intellect with their potential power and downfall.

We are warned to be cautious with the Tree of Knowledge of Good and Evil for 'eating' unwisely from it will result in 'death'.

The gifts of conscious awareness and intellect are powerful. They are our freedom for they give us the power to know ourselves and our world and consequently, the power to be co-creators of ourselves and the planet. However, these gifts can only be effective if we stay connected to the Tree of Life[8]. For only then

---

[8]'Staying connected with the Tree of Life' means staying connected to the Source of Life within us and without us and revere life with its nature and experiences

we can live fully, use the capacity for consciousness and judgement wisely, and be guided towards that which is loving, compassionate, and true ('good').

When we disconnect from the Tree of Life we inevitably fall into undue judgement of 'good' and 'bad' – we judge ourselves, others, and life unwisely and unlovingly. It is a judgement that comes from the intellect, from 'ego', and from arrogance, fear, need, or insecurity rather than from the God Within and Without. We become destructive co-creators of ourselves and the planet.

The 'punishment' of death symbolises the consequence of forgetting these truths that were understood at the very 'beginning - The resulting damage to our lives, the lives of others, and to our planet, is indeed a process of 'dying' on all levels...

Conclusions

Judaism existed well before Abraham and the Jewish People; it existed at the very beginning, it was what was clearly understood, realized, and lived by.

Judaism belonged with all life, with all humanity...

Back to the story of Judaism and the Jewish People

Genesis tells us humans lost Judaism. They slowly forgot and disconnect from certain truths; they became more and more distanced from the Tree of Life and fell more and more into the pitfalls contained in the Tree of Knowledge of Bad and Evil. 'Spiritual death' and decay replaced truth, knowledge, and inner and outer connection. The Oneness of the Source of Life was forgotten and with it all other truths became lost and were replaced with 'separateness' and with 'Gods' who were feared and believed to be separate from humans.

One man – Noah - did not entirely forget and kept some connection with these truths. However, Noah is not regarded as the 'father' of the Jewish People. A 9th generation descendant of his son Shem – a man called Abram – received this 'title'. Why? How did Abram differ from Noah?

The story of Abram begins with his father – Terach - who lived in Ur Kasdim - believed to be in North Mesopotamia which is Turkey today. Terach had three sons - Abram, Nachor and Haran.

- Abram, the eldest was married to Saray who did not bear him children.
- Nachor, the middle son, had a wife who bore him eight children and a mistress who gave him three more.
- Haran, the youngest, died at a young age, he was buried in Ur Kasdim and left behind a son – Lot.

Terach wanted a new start. He took his son Abram, his daughter-in-law Saray and his grandson Lot and together they journeyed to the land of Canaan (known today as Lebanon, Syria, Jordan, and Israel). It was a desirable place to live in due to its fertile soil and resources and its strategic location.

The land of Canaan was not a consolidated land but split into small city-states each with a king and each attempting to expand at the expense of its neighbour. This struggle was concurrent with external competition from larger powers who wanted to dominate the area. It may be due to the volatility of the area or to another reason that Terach and his family's journey ended in the city of Haran located on the Syrian border with Turkey - about 10 miles north of their destination.

This is where they settled and where Terach died.

It was after the death of Terach that Abram set out on an inner journey of awakening and transformation. We know this because the writer used time appropriate terminology and language to indicate that a transformation was taking place. We are told that Abram began to be guided and motivated by 'the voice of God', by dreams, visions, and premonitions. In today's terminology we would say that Abram began to awaken, to turn inwardly and listen to his truer deeper inner voice. He began to re-connect with and pay attention to his Essence - the 'God Within' - and inevitably he also began to reconnect with the 'God Without' of which this Essence is a part.

In a world where 'Judaism' was lost, where humans lost inner and outer connection, forgot the Oneness of the Source of Life, fell into separateness, feared and worshiped many 'Gods' believed to be separate from humans - Abram glimpsed once more the truths of Oneness, of One Source[9]. He did not simply choose one God above all others, he began to recon-nect with the truth of One Source of all life, to recognize his relationship with this One Source both within him and without him, to re-connect with the unity, oneness and interconnect-edness that underlies all life, and to re-experience the beauty, goodness, reverence, and moral precept that come with this connection.

To this awakening awareness of One Source within and without Abram made an unchangeable commitment.

---

[9]One Source is one of the many descriptive terms including: Greater Source, God, the God Without and Universe, Greater Essence etc for the Oneness. They all refer to The Source of all life. 'God' is a symbolic archetype image/name to this Source.

Abram took this personal commitment one step further - He made it not only on his own behalf but also on behalf of his descendants for generations to come and became the 'founding father' of the Jewish People – his descendants – and they became the 'Chosen People':

'Chosen' to keep the commitment to continue the journey of awakening to the truth of the Oneness; to stay true to this truth with its beauty, goodness and moral precept and live by it; to keep it alive within themselves and for all humanity and ensure it is never lost again.

It was not 'God' that chose Abram and his descendants, but Abram who chose 'God' for himself and his descendants...

Here Abram differs from Noah, for while Noah made a personal commitment only, Abram made both a personal and a collective commitment.

Abram's commitment coupled with a calling to manifest his father's vision to make the land of Canaan 'Home' - A 'Home' where he could settle and grow in numbers to become a people with a place of their own from where they could fulfil their commitment and ensure that what was given to humanity from the beginning of times remained alive and would not be lost.

This is the beginning of the story of reawakening Judaism and of the Jewish People's aspiration for a land where their commitment to this ongoing reawakening could be lived and fulfilled.

Abram's journey towards spiritual growth continued as he allowed 'the voice of God', dreams, premonitions, and inspiration (i.e. the voice of inner guidance) to guide him:

- He leaves Haran with his wife Saray, his nephew Lot and all his household and fulfilled his aspiration to settle in the part of the land of Canaan that is today Israel & West Bank.

  To express his gratitude and re-enforce his commitment, he builds an altar.

- Soon after settling in Canaan, Abram was finally blessed with the birth of a son - Ishmael - meaning 'the Lord has listened'. Ishmael was born to Hagar -an Egyptian mistress 'given' to Abram by Saray to compensate for being unable to bear him children (as was customary in those days). Ishmael was endowed with a blessing to father a Nation.

- In accordance with the vision that he will father many nations and his descendants will inhabit the land of Canaan for generations to come, Abram's name is changed to Abraham = 'father of many nations' in Hebrew.

- There is a calling for Abraham to express his commitment to the Oneness of all life with the symbolic act of circumcision.

  Circumcision was a common practice in those days for the purposes of hygiene (to prevent disease when bathing was not easily accessible), as a rite of passage, and as a form of religious sacrifice. Abraham embraced this tradition with all its purposes as a symbol to the commitment he made on behalf of himself and his descendants.

  He circumcised every male of his household, including himself and his son Ishmael and bound his descendants to continue this practice and circumcise newborn males on their eighth day of life. The choice of the eighth day of life symbolizes the day after the first week of life - six days of 'creation'/ 'evolution', followed by the seventh day of rest, the Shabbat.

- Another important indication of Abraham's spiritual awakening and transformation is the story of the destruction of Sedom and Gamora. We are told of Abraham's 'discussion' with God insisting that the good must not perish with the bad.

  This reflects a growing recognition of the Oneness underlying all life and the inevitable reverence for all life that comes with it – for Abraham insists to look for, focus on and preserve the good, even as the darkness exists.

  It also reflects a growing realization of one's relationship with one's Soul and its Source (the God Without), 'blind obedience' gives way to discipline coupled with reflection.

Saray also goes through her own process of awakening and transformation. She too begins to be guided by 'the voice of God', by dreams and visions – indicating that she is attuning inwards.

Like Abraham, Saray is called to change her name to Sara (meaning noble ruling lady in Hebrew).

She has a vision of bearing a son at which she laughs at due to her infertility and age. But her vision materializes, and she is guided to call her son Yzhaq (meaning 'laughing' in Hebrew) and as per his commitment Abraham circumcised Yzhaq on his eighth day of life.

Like his half-brother Ishmael, Yzhaq too was endowed with the blessing of fathering a Great Nation yet a clear distinction was made between Ishmael's and Yzhaq's descendants:

It was Yzhaq's not Ishmael's descendants who were to bear the responsibility for carrying forth Abraham's covenant with God[10], for marking this commitment with the act of circumcision, and to inherit the part of the land of Canaan that Abraham inhabited (Israel and West Bank).

Such distinction was not uncommon at the time; a man could differentiate between a son born to him from his wife and a son born to him from a mistress. It was also customary for a wife, once bearing her husband a child, to request that her husband's mistress and the children she birthed to him, be sent away - as Sarah did. Hence, Yzhaq and Ishmael were separated – each to their own destiny.

Hagar -the mistress – and her son Ishmael were not sent empty handed. Abraham provided them food and supplies and took them south of Canaan - known today as the Sinai Desert, Egypt, and Arabia - where he re-settled them, and where they flourished. Ishmael grew to be a hunter. His mother Hagar took him a wife and mistresses from Egypt, and he was blessed with 25 children. He lived in the desert and died at a ripe old age leaving behind an expanded household that, as promised, was the seed of a Nation – the People of Arabia.

Yzhaq stayed in the north-west parts of the land of Canaan and his descendants - the Jewish People – were left to carry on Abraham's commitment.

Abraham indeed became the father of many nations – Arab and Jewish – paternal siblings who seem to be forever in a rift.

---

[10]God here refers to both the God Within - the flame that we are - and its source, the Greater God Without.

Spiritual awakening does not come easy, old ways always lurk in the shadows to pull one back into darkness and it was no different for Abraham...

A few years into Yzhaq's childhood Abraham heard what he believed to be 'the voice of God' (an inner calling) instructing him to take Yzhaq to a specific mountain, build an altar and sacrifice him. This was a moment of truth for Abraham because what he really heard was the voice and pull of old pagan ways and conditioning – the custom to sacrifice one's child to the 'Gods' and the culture of 'blind obedience'. Just when it seemed that Abraham succumbed to 'old ways' he was pulled back by another inner call not to harm the child. This was Abraham's moment of triumph as he took a giant step forward to break ties with old pagan ways and most importantly, learn to differentiate a true inner calling from a false one and the true Divine within and without from the false and conditioned one. However, Abraham's journey of awakening to the underlying unity and Oneness was far from complete, he still felt the need to make a 'life sacrifice' and replaced his son Yzhaq with a lamb[11].

We do not know much about Abraham's journey following this event except that after Sara's death and as Yzhaq reached adulthood, Abraham finds him a suitable wife - Rivka - before departing himself and passing on his blessings, realizations, and the commitment to continue the journey to Yzhaq and his descendants.

---

[11] It is unfortunate that the story of Yzhaq sacrifice is still interpreted and taught as 'God' testing Abraham's loyalty rather than as a recognition of Abraham's spiritual growth journey as he learns to realize the true nature of 'God' and the process of letting go of old conditioning. Such interpretation discredits the very core of Judaism and the Source of Life itself...

Yzhaq's life seemed uneventful. We are not told of major personal realizations or events that had a collective impact on the Jewish story till close to his death when, as was customary at the time, he was to offer his blessings to his and Rivka's twin sons - Eisav and Jacob.

Eisav was the eldest by moments and therefore was entitled to the eldest son's blessing however, the blessings were given to Jacob instead. This 'calamity' was due partly to a 'foolish' moment when Eisav sold his 'eldest son's rights' to Jacob, and partly to Rivka who believed Jacob to be a more suitable candidate for the eldest son blessings and encouraged him to trick his old father who was blind into believing he was Eisav.

The significance of this event was that –

First, it was now Jacob and his descendants who were given both the blessing and the responsibility to carry on Abraham's commitment.

Second, as with Ishmael and Yzhak another sibling rift impacted on the Jewish People: 'Licking his wounds' Eisav went to the south of Canaan. He found his peace by marrying one of his 'half uncle' – Ishmael - daughters and a few 'local women'. His descendants joined and expanded the Arab world and deepened the rift between it and the Jewish People whose story now continues with Jacob...

Eisav's anger and desire for revenge caused Jacob to flee the land of Canaan. He was sent by his ageing parents - Yzhaq and Rivka - to safety with his uncle Lavan (Rivka's brother). It was a physical journey that marked the start of Jacob's spiritual journey and inevitably, the ongoing awakening and unfolding of Judaism and the Jewish story. Like his grandfather Abraham, Jacob's life was rich with lessons, realizations, transformations and enforcement of the commitment that was now entrusted upon him and his descendants - A commitment to keep moving towards the realization of Oneness and towards living in alignment with its guide within and without.

Jacob's spiritual journey begins with a dream where he was reminded of the commitment at hand and assured of his safety and prosperity while keeping true to it. Like his grandfather Abraham and as was then customary Jacob honoured and enforced his commitment by building an altar of thanks before continuing his journey.

On arrival to his uncle Lavan he was well received but had to learn the lesson of the pain of deceit and betrayal. After working for seven years with the promise to marry Lavan's younger daughter - his beloved Rachel - he was given Leah, the eldest daughter instead and had to work another seven years to finally marry her younger sister, Rachel.

Nevertheless, Jacob spent 20 years with his uncle and his household prospered both in material wealth and in number for he was blessed with 11 sons and a number of daughters born to him by his two wives and the mistresses given to him by them as they competed for his affection.

After 20 years Jacob felt called to return to Canaan - The land of his birth, of Yzahq his father and Abraham his grandfather, the land he had to flee because of his brother's rage and where he and his descendants were to live the commitment entrusted to them, and his journey back home begins. It is a journey with more lessons and transformation:

1. First, he needed to learn the lesson of negotiation-
   He had to find a way to amicably part from his uncle (now also father-in-law) and separate their two prosperous households fairly.
   He also needed to reconcile with his brother Eisav.
   Amid fears of these challenges, and prayers to manage them well, Jacob had many dreams and visions enforcing the message of his safety and welcoming him back to the land of Canaan.
2. Second, like his grandfather Abraham he was called to change his name from Jacob to Israel (meaning in Hebrew - the inspiration of the Divine dwells with thee) and his descendants became known as the Israelites...
3. Third, just before he and his household reached their destination – the land of Canaan -Israel had to learn the pain of personal loss. Rachel, his beloved wife, lost her life while giving birth to a son - Benjamin - his 12th and last son. He built an altar to mark his gratitude for his son and the pain of losing his wife before finally re-entering Canaan with his 12 sons = The Israelites.

There was yet another chapter of loss, recovery, and growth.

Israel had a favourite child - Joseph - the eldest child given to him by his beloved Rachel who had difficulties conceiving. This fondness displeased Joseph's siblings and problems escalated with Joseph's ongoing dreams of grandeur. Revengefully, his siblings sold Joseph into slavery to merchants who travelled to

Egypt and covered their actions by telling their father, Israel, that Joseph was taken by a wild beast.

Joseph's destiny smiled at him. What had angered his siblings - his dreams and his ability to interpret them - now served him well as he was called upon to interpret the Pharaoh's re-occurring dreams. The interpretations pleased Pharaoh and Joseph was made his permanent advisor.

All the while, Israel and his remaining 11 sons continued living in Canaan with their households growing, expanding, and prospering. But a harsh famine forced them to travel to Egypt that thanks to Joseph's dreams interpretations was well prepared for the famine. Israel, his sons, and their households were re-united with Joseph and were forgiven and granted permission to stay in Egypt as Pharaoh's subjects during the famine. This security came at a price - the land of Canaan was now lost to them because as Pharaoh's subjects they could now only leave with his permission.

Israel (Jacob) died in Egypt after blessing each of his 12 sons. A special permission was granted by Pharaoh for Joseph to follow his father Israel last wish and transfer his bones to the land of Canaan – the land of his birth, of his father Yzaque and his grandfather Abraham, the land to which his descendants will hopefully return one day...

As for the Israelites, their 'luck' changed following the death of the Pharaoh who knew them. A new and hostile Pharaoh who felt threatened by their growth and prosperity came to power. He enslaved the Israelites and used them as manpower to build pyramids, palaces etc. This slavery lasted for 400years until Moses was born to an Israelite man and his wife.

Moses' future looked dim for the Pharaoh ordered all new-born males Israelites to be killed. In an attempt to save her son, Moses' mother sent him in a small boat across the Nile to be 'found' by the Pharaoh's daughter who would hopefully take pity on him and save him, as happened and Moses was raised in the palace. Nevertheless, something remained within him... As a young adult he took pity on the Israelites and when he saw an Israelite treated harshly by an Egyptian guard, he killed the guard and secretly buried him. This action had severe consequences, not only was his identity revealed to him and all, but also the Pharaoh was furious and demanded revenge. Moses' time in the palace was over and his journey began...

Moses escaped to Midian - a land south of Egypt - where he settled as a humble shepherd, found a wife, and had a family. Although comfortable, he felt like a stranger in the land and his heart called him back to his enslaved people in Egypt. However, only when the Pharaoh in whose palace he was raised died, and after he had a vision reminding him of his true identity, of the commitment made by his ancestors, and of the promised land prior to descending to Egypt, did he follow the calling... The story of the Israelites exodus from Egypt under the leadership of Moses, his brother Aaron, and his sister Miriam began...

Moses' job was overwhelming and much more than just leading the exodus because:

1. The Israelites loss of independence after 400years of slavery meant that a new spirit of independence needed to be installed.

2. After 400years of slavery in Egypt, some old 'pagan' ways of Egyptian culture had filtered into the Israelites lives replacing the awakening journey that began with their fore-fathers. Moses had the task of reviving within each individual, and within the people collectively, the journey of awakening, the once glimpsed Oneness and unity with its beauty, goodness, and moral precept, and the commitment to continue the journey.

3. Not only the Israelites – the descendants of Israel - were led out of Egypt. With them came many others who were enslaved in Egypt but were not Israelites. They had faith in Moses, Aaron, and Miriam and wanted to free themselves and build a new life in a new land with the Israelites. They were mostly pagans who knew nothing of the Israelites commitment to journey towards the Oneness and unity of all life. Moses not only had the task of uniting the Israelites and non-Israelites into one people/ nation, but also of forging in the non-Israelites a spirit and a commitment that was totally foreign and unknown to them.

These facts shed light on two dilemmas in the story of the Jewish People.

It explains the mystery of the 40 years journey from Egypt across the Sinai. It does not take 40 years to physically cross from Egypt to Canaan, but it does take 40 years to –

- Purge the culture of slavery,
- Rekindle Abraham's journey of awakening within the Israelites,
- Introduce this commitment to the non-Israelites.

It does take 40 years to forge a united people of individuals willing to be true and committed to –

- The ongoing journey of awakening,
- The truth of Oneness underlying all life,
- The unity of Source,
- The beauty and goodness that emanates from these truths,
- Make these truths a daily living reality,
- Serve as a model to others...

Achieving all this required the old generation to be replaced with a new one - hence 40years.

It also explains how and why the Jewish People's prescribed path – Judaism's 'package deal' was created.

The people needed 'road signs' to support them and Moses drafted 613 commandments and related practices - including the Ten Commandments aiming to unite them, to bring them into covenant, ensure they remember their story and commitment, and serve as stepping-stones in the ongoing journey of awakening to the spirit of Oneness and to the reverence for life.

The commandments and related practices provided a 'how to' for remembering and for daily living, ways of behaving and being that covered every aspect of human life (as it then was) and attempted to elevate life as much as was possible at the time. They offered deep messages about life, its Source, being human and relating to all life.

It is however vital to acknowledge the following factors with regards to the commandments:

1. First, because Moses needed to bring into covenant a people who were under pagan influences either because they lost connection with Abraham's realized Oneness (the Israelites) or because they never had connection to it (the non-Israelites), he may have needed to include some 'compromises' in his 613 commandments (hence the words 'as much as was possible at the time').

2. Second, some of these commandments may have been added by the Priests, or other leaders, of the time after Moses passing (refer to p.40).

3. Third, the commandments shifted Judaism from being -

   A personal and collective commitment to the ongoing journey of awakening to the truth of Oneness through inner connectedness and guidance, whereby the Oneness and all that entails from it act as a compass with which one aligns.

   To being -

   A path of commandments with their underlying messages through which the awakening to the truth of Oneness can take place and through which it can be preserved and protected.

   This path serves Judaism to-date and will be further explored in following chapters.

With the imparting of the commandments Moses mission was completed ... He too was too old to enter Abraham's promised land - the land of Canaan - but was rewarded for his work by being able to view the land from the top of the mountain before passing away peacefully and leaving the task of leading the new generation with a younger leader – Joshua...

The Torah (the first five books of the Old Testament) concludes with Moses' passing.

The remaining books of the Bible tell us of the continuing history of Judaism and the Jewish People including the Israelites entry and settlement in Canaan; the building of a kingdom under Judges and Kings; the separation of the kingdom following Solomon's death, by his sons to Israel and Judea; the fall of Israel to Babylon and the exile of the Israelites; and later the fall of Judea[12] and the destruction of the first Temple.

The story of Judaism and the Jewish People does not end with the collapse of the first Temple. It continues well beyond the Bible with the partial return to the land of Canaan (Israel), the construction of the second Temple and its capture and collapse under the Roman Empire and the second exile. It takes another two thousand years in exile with some prosperity but mostly persecutions and a tragic holocaust before the Jewish People finally return to their home – Canaan = Israel...

This is the story of the Jewish People and Judaism.

A Light unto the Nations

It is essential to address the notion of the Jewish People as 'the chosen people' and as 'a light unto the nation' because it is often misunderstood by non-Jews and Jews alike to be an expression of 'spiritual superiority' or of privilege. Nothing could be further from the truth. 'Chosen people' and 'being a light unto the nation'

---

[12]Following the separation of the kingdom to Israel and Judea and the fall of Israel to Babylon, the Israelites become known as The Jewish People – the People of Judea – the remaining kingdom...

are expressions of the responsibility imparted by Abraham on his descendants both individually and collectively.

This responsibility is an individual and collective choice to stay true and committed to Abraham's journey of awakening to the truth of Oneness of Source and all life and all that entails from it, and to live by it daily as best as is possible.

Staying true and committed to this journey has spiritual and practical implication on the way one lives and behaves in the world. It shines from within and without and impacts one's inner and outer reality. It keeps the journey alive, so it is never again forgotten nor lost to humanity and is hopefully, followed by others.

The notion of 'the chosen people' and 'being a light unto nations' is an expression of a commitment to lead by example.

- It is not an act of arrogant superiority but of humble service.
- It is not a privilege but a responsibility.
- It is not an act of enforcing upon others but rather of being that which one wants the world to be.
- It is not because the Jewish People are 'better than others' but because they agreed to take on the commitment to stay true to awakening to, and being guided by, the truth of the Oneness so that they can be their very best any time, in any situation, and in all aspect of life. By doing so they allow the Oneness to manifest, shine, be seen and remembered by all.

Some Jews (and non-Jews) may object to the notion of the Jewish People carrying an individual and collective responsibility 'to be a role model'.

They may say that every human being must live as they do for themselves and not for the purpose of being a 'role model.' It is true that each human can live as they choose, but it is not true that it is for oneself only. Whatever we humans do or not do, and however each of us choses to live will have an impact - we never live for ourselves only!

They may say that it is the responsibility of each human to be role model and not just a 'Jewish' responsibility. It is true that each human being shares this very same responsibility, for it is our innate human calling. Nevertheless, every Jew carries this responsibility not only as part of their human calling, but also as part of their Jewish calling, for they are part of a people entrusted with keeping this responsibility alive for all humanity. This is not an expression of 'superiority' but of an added responsibility. The Jewish commitment for 'Tikun Olam' (repairing the world) stems from the notion of 'being a light unto the nations'. It is the responsibility every Jew carries to contribute towards making the world a better place in however small or big way.

They may say that this notion is arrogant because the world is full of non-Jews who were/ are wonderful role models from whom we can learn and follow. It is true that the world is full of past and present committed humans who are not of the Jewish religion and have much to teach us. One does not have to be Jewish to be an excellent role model, it is a collective human calling. This truth does not remove the responsibility of every Jew to serve and be a role model.

Wanting to dismiss this task and responsibility or perceiving it as arrogant is mistaken, especially when such dismissal and perception come from within the Jewish community. It discredits the very nature of the commitment of Judaism and it can result in the individual and collective stumbling of the Jewish People.

The paradox is that despite all these objections, from within, Jewish people tend to have high expectations of themselves both individually and collectively and put themselves under personal and collective ongoing self-scrutiny and self-criticism. From without, even though often criticized for seeing themselves as 'chosen' and/or 'superior', Jewish people are under constant scrutiny. They are the most criticized of all people and nations and there seem to be an unspoken expectation that they behave and act in the light of the highest moral stance. What other individuals and/or nations may 'get away with', they – be it individually or collectively – are often harshly criticized for! This is the responsibility with which every Jew and the Jewish People collectively were entrusted. This is the very nature of their unchangeable commitment to stay true to the journey of awakening to the truth of Oneness, live by it daily as best as is possible, and lead by example.

This responsibility and commitment provided in the past and provides in the present a pillar of personal and collective strength and a reverence for life that supports the survival of Judaism and the Jewish People...

Faith or Betrayal

With the story of Judaism revealed, 'what it means to be Jewish' also unveiled and it was time to choose between 'faith' and 'betrayal'...

Through my personal inner journey- of *'To Life'*- I came to re-connect with what I always knew was there and true:

- The truth of Oneness and the realization of the underlying unity of all life, and that all life emanates from the One Source.
- The recognition that everyone and everything that exists - including me - are a 'flame' of this One Source. A Source that is within each of us, within everything and everyone, and is who I really am and who all existence really is.
- The realization that I and everyone (and everything) are at essence love, intelligence and freedom manifesting in a special way through each of us, shining within us and waiting to guide us to live wisely, lovingly, and creatively - we just need to be still, aware and listen.
- The awareness of the beauty, goodness and moral precept that comes from all these truths.
- The sanctification of all life (of everyone and everything), even in the midst of darkness.
- The realization of the nature of humanity with its potential for full consciousness and the gifts of this potential as its lurking pitfalls.
- The recognition of truths such as the creative and destructive power of the word; the beauty and vitality of allocating time for silence, gratitude, reflection, and enjoyment (Shabbat) and much more.

These are all at the very core of Judaism. My personal journey allowed me to see and reconnect with Judaism's true diamond. As I made a personal unchangeable commitment to stay on the journey of awakening and to keep moving towards the Oneness and all the truths entailing from it, I felt in perfect alignment with Abraham and Judaism's quest and commitment. My inner connection with Judaism came alive and I could declare a renewed faith to its story and commitment.

On the other hand, the source of my unease with Judaism also became clear. It came from Judaism's 'package deal' - A 'Package Deal' that governs many behaviours, attitudes, and practices within Judaism and of the Jewish People. All forms of Judaism and all Jewish People whether Orthodox, Conservative, Traditional, Liberal, or Reform, have at least some reverence for it and follow it to a lesser or greater extent. It is a 'package deal' with eternal messages, as with messages and practices relevant for a specific time only. Pondering the Jewish People relationship with Judaism's 'Package Deal' had to be the next step. Doing so will not only further clarify the unease, but also support the exploration of questions such as:

- How does Judaism and the Jewish People 'behave' in the world in relation to other religions? Is there disrespect, intolerance and imposing?
- Do Jewish People behave in a way that is true to 'being a light unto the nations'?
- Are they true to the truth of Oneness?

Chapter 10:
The Jewish People & Judaism's 'Package Deal'

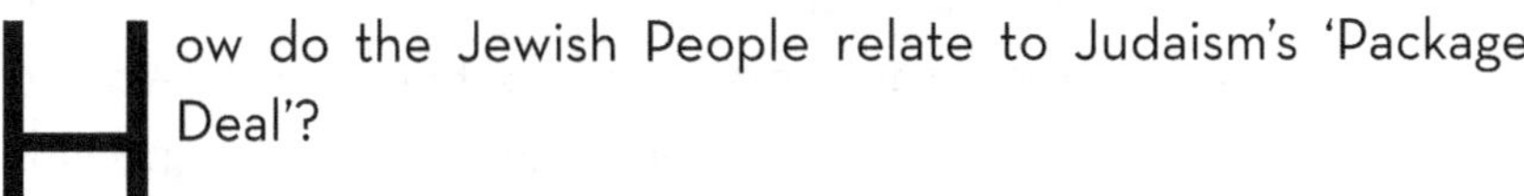

How do the Jewish People relate to Judaism's 'Package Deal'?

- Does the 'package deal' support living the realized truths and the commitment to them?
- Is the 'package deal' rigid or open?
- Does it keep the commitment alive or suffocate it?
- Have the realized truths become 'lost' in the 'package deal'?

These questions require recalling that –

1. 'Package deal' refers to an established system of practices put in place to express, bring into daily living, and keep alive an unchangeable commitment to certain realized truths.

2. Judaism existed well before its forefathers. There was no 'package deal' but a recognition of and commitment to the truth of Oneness of Source and all life, and all that stems from this truth.

This continued to be the case with the Jewish People forefathers' - Abraham, Yzaque, Jacob - and their households. They also did not have a 'package deal'. They had a commitment to stay true to the ongoing journey of awakening to the fundamental truth of Oneness of Source and life - A Truth with which they re-connected.

This journey simply asked them to allow the truth of Oneness and the commitment to it shine in their hearts and be their true inner voice and guide them in the 'how to' of everyday living. This allowed them to be the best version of themselves and give their best. The more they listened to this inner voice, the more it strengthened and evolved within them and the more it manifested outwardly and was seen by others who would hopefully follow. The only practices to which they committed were the symbolic act of circumcision, honouring the Shabbat as a day of rest and gratitude, and adhering to the values that stemmed naturally from the truth of Oneness.

This was the 'original' form of Judaism.

However, Moses changed this because he had to...

He needed to forge a united people of the Israelites and non- Israelites who accompanied them. A united people connected and committed to Abraham's, Yzaque's and Jacob's ongoing journey of awakening to the truth of Oneness.

Moses needed to revive and re-connect this truth and commitment within the Israelites themselves, for it had become lost to them in 400 years of slavery and exposure to pagan practices. They needed a 'package deal' suitable to their time through which they could re-connect with the once glimpsed truths and re-commit to the ongoing journey of awakening to them – A 'package deal' to support 'Home Coming' and the ongoing journey.

He also needed to instil in the non-Israelites the spirit of the truth of Oneness and a commitment to be true to the ongoing journey of awakening to it - A spirit and commitment that was essentially foreign and unknown to them. They even more than the Israelites needed a 'package deal'- A 'how to'.

Consequently, Judaism 'package deal' was created and Judaism shifted from being a path of –

A personal and collective commitment to the ongoing journey of awakening to the truth of Oneness of Source and Life by means of inner connectedness and guidance that is always aligned with the Oneness,

To being -

A path of commandments (a 'package deal' of 'how to') with their underlying messages through which the journey of awakening to the truth of Oneness of Source and Life can take place, and the commitment to it can be preserved.

A 'package deal' can be helpful, even necessary at times, to support connection to one's history, support commitment to one's truths and their daily living and preservation. Judaism's 'package deal' offers all these. It offers stepping-stones to the journey of awakening and acts as a constant reminder of this commitment and keeps it alive. It brings this commitment into everyday living with 'traditions', 'symbolic acts' and 'practices that carry important messages and bring individuals together to create a united People who remember their history and are committed to this journey.

Nevertheless, as we now know, it is essential to recognize that:

1. A 'package deal' is always a means to an end never an end to itself. One must avoid making the 'package deal' the focus rather than the truths it aims to express and preserve, and there must always be room left for varied expression and for growth and evolvement. The same is true and must apply to Moses' commandments.

2. A 'package deal' must always be seen in the context of its time (i.e. language, culture etc) and purpose, and in the context of its alignments with the truths upon which it is founded and which it aims to express and preserve. Judaism's 'package deal' must therefore be seen not only in the context of its time, but also in the context of its alignment with the truth of Oneness upon which it is founded and to which it is committed. The Oneness is its true guiding compass.

Moses understood this.

He understood that while his 'package deal' of 613 commandments had achieved its immediate purpose as a collective uniting value; as a guide to revive within the Israelites the commitment to their forefathers' truths; and as a way to introduce these truths to the non-Israelites - They were only the beginning of the journey, not its conclusion...

He understood that if his 'package deal' was to continue to reflect its intended messages and to act as a powerful guide to the ongoing journey of awakening to the truth of Oneness for generations to come, it must always be seen in the light of its alignment with this truth, in the context of the language, terminology, and culture of its time, and in accordance with its intended purpose. Moses instructed the Israelites not to change the words he left them with, not to add nor subtract from them not because he wanted the 'package deal' to become 'frozen in time' but on the contrary, because he knew that only by leaving the words just as they were, would it be possible in the future to see them in the light of their alignment with the truth of Oneness and in the context of their time. Then, their intended meaning, their true purpose and message can be seen and carried - as high as possible - into the future in alignment with the evolvement of life and humanity.

Seeing Judaism' 'package deal' in the light of its alignment with the truth of Oneness and in the context of its time is also the tool needed to expose commandments and related practices that were most likely given by Moses to 'pacify' and bring into cove-nant Israelites who may have adapted some foreign ways and the non-Israelites; and commandments that were added after Moses' passing by the Priests and other leaders of the time for their specific – most likely self-serving - purpose (refer to p50).

This is where Judaism sometimes leaves me and other fellow Jews wanting...

Within too many sectors of Judaism we see an adherence which can be rigid, 'blind' and refuses to see the commandments in the context of their alignment with the truth of Oneness and in the context of their purpose and the culture of their time; refuses to acknowledge life and humanity as it was at the time, the possible 'foreign' influences, and the possible self-serving 'additions.' An adherence where practices become an 'end' unto themselves; where they neither leave room for 'individual guidance' and freedom of expression, nor for the evolvement of life and humanity... Instead, they inhibit growth in consciousness, and they become devoid of their intended meaning and underlying truth.

Paradoxically, such adherence sabotages what it intends to protect - The ongoing journey of awakening to the truth of Oneness. It obscures the diamond of the commandments and damages the essential elements upon which Judaism of our forefathers was founded.

I recognize the right and freedom of every Jew to freely practice in the manner they choose, and most importantly, in the way they are guided – Inner guidance is at the very essence of Judaism. Nevertheless –

- A practice that is rigid becomes an end to itself rather than a means to an end.
- A failure to see any commandment and its related practices in the light of its alignment with the truth of Oneness and in the context of time - is a problem because:
  - o The deeper and eternal truths underlying a commandment and its related practices - truths aimed at re-kindling connection with the truth of Oneness and all that entails from it - are lost.
  - o Practices that may have taken people's journey towards the Oneness 2000 years ago, can now become an obstacle that hinders the journey.
  - o It hinders the capacity to expose commandments and related practices included as a 'necessary compromise' at

the time or added later by the Priests (the Kohanim and Levitis), or whoever else.

Only when commandments and their related practices are recognized as a means to an end, when they are aligned with the Oneness and seen in the context of time, can they be unveiled for what they are, and can their deeper eternal truth be recognized.

Only when they are unveiled and their truth recognized can one see whether it is relevant to leave a certain practice as is, find a new way to serve its message, allow it to evolve and reach a higher place, or let go of. More still, one recognizes that there may be different ways to serve any message, what remains important is staying true to the underlying truth and the intended message, moving towards it, expressing it, and living it in freedom.

And then can Judaism become once more as intended by our forefathers:

An unchangeable commitment to the ongoing journey of awakening to the truth of Oneness of Source and all life with its beauty, goodness, and moral percept.

A commitment and a truth with which we are each connected, which shines in our heart and is lived daily as we allow it to speak, be our inner voice and guide.

A commitment and a truth for which, the commandments - aligned with the Oneness and seen in the context of time - can act as a guiding compass that reminds us and reconnects us if we are lost or are unsure.

Then, we can live, be and give our best each moment, we can shine within and without and be a 'model' to others.

This is the journey and the commitment that we pass on to our descendants.

Judaism' Package Deal'

In the forthcoming chapters, the commandments with their related practices and how we relate to them will be explored. While it is not possible in this book to explore 613 commandments and related practices, it is helpful to group them into themes and to explore the themes most relevant in answering to the question of Judaism and the Jewish People in the World at present.

I have grouped the commandments into seven themes with the first five being:

- *Relationship to Source (God)* – This theme includes prayers and blessings, signs and symbols and one's relationship to the Torah and the commandments.
- *Inter human relationships* - Commandments regarding brotherhood - Jews relating to other Jews and to non-Jews, relating to the poor and unfortunate, relationships with employees, slaves, and servants[13], business relationships, family, and gender relationships[14].
- *Times and Seasons* – Commandments regarding all celebrated Holy Days including the Shabbat and practices in relation to them.

---

[13]One must bear in mind the context of time and culture within which these commandments were offered, times when 'ownership' of slaves and servants was permitted.

[14]These include marriage, divorce, man-woman relation, and all sexual relations/ behaviours.

- *Dietary Laws* - Commandments relating to foods allowed and not allowed and practices regarding the treatment of the land, agriculture, and Animal Husbandry.
- *Specific behaviours* - These commandments refer to various human matters such as Oath, Vows, Prophecy, Idolatry, clothing, and War.

These five themes with their commandments and practices are the most relevant today and will be explored in the forthcoming chapters.

The remaining two themes are:

- *The Court and law system* - Commandments and practices regarding the process of the Court and the appointment of judges and witnesses. They also include criminal laws and laws in relation to injuries and damages, to property and property rights and to punishment and restitution.
- *The Temple* – Commandments regarding matters such as the Kohanim/Levites (the priests), the Nazarites (the monks), Temple practices, donations and taxes, Temple Sanctuary and Sacrifices.

Both these themes with their commandments and practices hold less relevance today.

The Court and Law System commandments and practices evolved more than any of the others. This is due to two factors. First, Jews living outside Israel abide by the laws of their country of residence. Second, in Israel, although the commandments relating to the law and court system have an impact on the country's Law and Court System, they are, to an extent, seen in the context of their time and of their deeper underlying message. Although Israel is a Jewish State, 'State' and 'Religion' are 'separated'. Also, since some strict Orthodox claim that 'messianic Israel' does not yet exist and therefore the 'court system and law' as given cannot be applied, they may have put less pressure to comply.

The Temple and its related commandments are not functional since the third Temple has yet not been rebuilt. This theme contains over 200 commandments and practices - one third of the total number of commandments! - and most likely includes many 'later-on' additions and 'foreign' influences.

Should pressure arise from streams within Judaism to review the Law and Court System and include more of the prescribed commandments, or should the Temple be re-built and there is a call to revive some of its related commandments and practices, it will be of the utmost importance to use the 'guiding compass' of alignment with the truth of Oneness and all that entails from it, and of the context of time and purpose.

It is absolutely necessary to use this 'guiding compass' when exploring all themes with their related commandments and practices. Failing to do so discredits Moses, discredits Abraham's, Yzaque's and Jacob's commitment, discredits Judaism itself and indeed, discredits the Source of Life itself.

Chapter 11:
Judaism and The Jewish People in the World

Do the Jewish People behave in ways that are disrespectful, intolerant, and impose on others?

Do they behave in ways that are true to being 'a light unto the nations'?

Are they true to the ongoing journey of awakening to the truth of Oneness?

These questions require us to reflect upon the Jewish People in relation to non-Jews and other religions, the inter-relation between Jews, and the Jewish People general behaviour.

The Jewish People in relation to non-Jews and other religions

How do the Jewish People behave towards other religions and the people who follow them?

History presents two contradictory facts:

- First, the Jewish People did not and do not enforce Judaism with its realized truths and commitment on others.

- Second, the Jewish People in the past and still today are unyielding in their choice to 'distinguish themselves from others' and are willing to protect and stand by their commitment to Judaism.

This was already apparent in biblical times. Although pagan practices were regarded as sinful and were rejected by the Israelites, there was no attempt to enforce the Oneness of Source and all life on pagan cultures. However, the Israelites purposefully distinguished themselves from all pagan cultures and were willing to fiercely defend and protect their truths and their commitment to them.

This attitude continued throughout history. Whatever situation the Jewish People found themselves in, while there was no attempt to enforce Judaism on others, there was a purposeful 'distinguishing from others' and an unyielding willingness to protect Judaism, either by 'active physical resistance' or by 'passive spiritual resistance' (such as keeping the faith internally while complying externally).

The same applies today. The Jewish People - whether orthodox, traditional, secular or reform - distinguish themselves from others and are willing to protect Judaism and their commitment to its realized truths, but not impose these truths on others. In my observation, a loss of faith in Judaism results not from losing faith in its truths but from not connecting with these truths through the 'prescribed path' (the 'package deal'). Those who search elsewhere, more often than not, search for these very same truths.

The motivation to 'distinguish from others' and to adhere to 'non enforcement' and 'unyielding protection' is rooted in a number of commandments.

On one hand, the Israelites were commanded to love the 'stranger' (Det.10:19) and not to wrong the 'stranger' in speech or deeds (Ex. 22:20).

On the other hand, they were commanded to distinguish themselves from pagan culture and practices and those who adhered to them, and to stay true to and protect the truth of Oneness of Source and life from such cultures. So important was 'distinguishing from idolatrous' and the prohibition of idolatry that 45 commandments warn of the severe consequences if one either practices or entices idolatry in any way (refer to Deut. 13&19; Ex. 23; & Lev. 18&19).

So fierce was the call for protection that the Israelites were commanded to clear the lands where they were to settle from all pagan places of worships (Deut. 12:2-3).

These commandments carry important messages:

1. One must not be afraid to be true to one's truth even if it differs from others and is not the more common shared truth – It is OK to distinguish from others.
2. Choosing to be 'different' and not share another's stand is not an invitation to disrespect or mistreat the other – One is called to 'love the stranger'.
3. 'Loving the stranger' does not mean 'being as the stranger' nor does it mean to refrain from protecting one's truth.
4. Protecting one's truth does not mean enforcing it on another.

These messages and truths are reflected in the Jewish People's behaviour towards non-Jews and other religions. They explain why the Jewish People did not 'enforce on others' while they protected and remained committed to the journey of awakening to the truth of Oneness of Source and all life, to living by it as best as possible at any time and allowing it to be seen by others so they can awaken to it in their own way.

Nevertheless, the Jewish People relationship to non-Jews and to other religions is not unblemished...

The commandment to 'distinguish from others' (refer to Deut. 13&19; Ex. 23; & Lev. 18&19).

'Distinguishing from others' simply implies not to be afraid to be true to one's truth. It is an expression of integrity, something we do with strongly held truths – truths that we have reflected on, have consciously chosen as our 'unchangeable truths', and we distinguish ourselves from others by remaining true to them.

The central commitment to Judaism is to stay true to the ongoing awakening to the truth of Oneness of Source and all life, to live this truth daily to the best of one's ability, and to keep it alive not only within oneself, but also for all to see and therefore, 'be a light unto the nations.' Jewish People are asked to 'distinguish from others' by remaining true to this commitment and not allowing others to steer them from it.

'Staying together' can provide a unity that sustains the ability of individuals and collectives to 'distinguish from others' and stay true to their purpose. It is an effective way of translating the commandment to 'distinguish from others' into practice.

However, all too often 'staying together' has been (and still is) translated by Jewish Communities into a culture of 'separating' or 'isolating' from others.' While this behaviour is not peculiar to the Jewish People only, it is not necessarily an effective practice and may not enhance their personal or collective purpose.

Through the lens of 'the context of time,' the practice of 'separating' from others may have been necessary for the Jewish People.

It may have been necessary for Abraham, Izhak, Jacob and their descendants (the Israelites) to 'stay together' by 'separating' and 'isolating' from the pagan cultures that surrounded them so they could 'distinguish themselves' and stay true to the journey of awakening.

It may have also been necessary following the exodus from Egypt. The Israelites needed to re-kindle their commitment to their forefathers' journey of awakening to the Oneness, and the non-Israelites who joined them needed to connect with this journey which was foreign to them. 'Staying together' by 'separating' and 'isolating' from others enabled them to 'distinguish' from and let go of idolatry and commit to the journey of awakening.

Likewise, the ongoing external intolerance and rejection of the Jewish People throughout history has put them in a 'defensive position'. The culture of 'staying together' by 'separateness' and 'isolation' sustained them and supported them so they could continue to 'distinguish themselves' and stay true to the journey of awakening.

To some extent this is still true today.

With all this being acknowledged, the question remains whether the culture of 'staying together' by 'isolating' and 'separating' from others really served the Jewish People and enhanced Judaism's vision, or whether while it seemed to have sustained them and Judaism, it was, and is now, damaging and hindering the progression of the journey of awakening.

It is the later that applies because a culture of 'staying together' by 'isolating' and 'separating' from others -

- Contradicts Judaism's truth of Oneness and the commitment to live by. There cannot be Oneness where there is 'separateness' and 'isolation', and one cannot live by this truth when one 'separates' and 'isolates' from others. Such culture renders the commitment to the Oneness untrue to itself.
- Contradicts the commitment to let the truth of Oneness shine within oneself for all to see and to 'be a light unto the nations.' How can one's light shine outwardly and be seen by others in 'separateness'? Separateness not only hides the light, but also does not foster a desire in others to follow.
- Perpetuates the cycle of 'separateness' as it creates an image of superiority and intolerance which invites an antagonistic rejection from others (non-Jews) to which Jews respond with more separation.
- Does not leave room for the full kaleidoscope of core truths to unveil (refer to 'Chapter 4'). How can the full kaleidoscope be seen when one shuts the door to others?

In the long run this practice is counter-productive, it results from -

- A failure to differentiate a given message from its practice,
- Allowing a practice to become the focus whilst losing the message,

- Failing to use the 'guiding compass' of alignment with the truth of Oneness and the context of time, nature, and purpose.

It may be time to learn new ways to 'distinguish from others', new ways of 'staying together' that sustain us without the damaging impact of 'isolation' and 'separateness'.

Doing so will support staying true to the journey of awakening and true to 'being a light unto the nations.' It will allow the journey of awakening to be seen and invite others to follow. It will also lead the way to demonstrate to other communities and individuals, effective ways to 'distinguish from others' while remaining loving to 'the stranger'.

The Commandment not to Cross-Marry (Deut. 7:3)

The Israelites were commanded not to marry with the 'gentile' (the non-Jew). 'Marrying out' (marrying a 'gentile') is still considered a form of betrayal not only by strict Orthodox Jews but also by many traditional Jews and even Secular Jews, which can result in a heartbreaking breakdown of families.

Is holding onto this commandment's rational as a strict rule rather than a guideline, effective? Does it benefit and promote Judaism today or does it –

- Promote a culture of 'separation' from others.
- Contradict Judaism's core spirit of Oneness and the commitment to live by it.
- Hinder the journey of awakening.
- Damage the commitment to 'be a light unto the nations'.
- Invite a perceived 'superiority' and antagonistic rejection from non-Jews to Jews.

The rationale for this commandment was the concern that "they (the non-Jews) turn away thy son from following me, that they (the Israelites) may serve other gods" (Deut. 7:4). It was feared such marriages would fail participants to 'distinguish from others' and Judaism would once more be lost...

In the context of its time, this commandment may have been effective. It was given to the Israelites at a time when they were vulnerable to the pagan cultures that surrounded them, and when the gap between pagan beliefs and Judaism was fundamental. Forbidding cross-marriage may have been a valid way of protecting the Israelites and ensuring they did not 'fall back' into practices that would pull them away from the Oneness and the commitment to it.

However, today the survival of Judaism is not subject to strict inter-marriage laws but to the Jewish People staying aligned with Judaism's held truths and commitment and steering away from all the pitfalls recognized in the first part of this book.

The paradox is that not only the Jewish forefathers – Abraham, Izhak and Jacob - had wives or mistresses many of whom came from non-Israelite cultures, but Moses who prescribed this commandment was himself married to Zipora – a woman from Midian, not an Israelite. Likewise, all but a few Jewish kings had non-Israelite wives or mistresses. And still, Judaism survived...

Was this commandment introduced by Moses or someone else? A commandment from Moses may rather state for one to marry a man/woman willing to respect their partner's commitment to the Oneness and embrace it...

Protecting Judaism by strict cross-marriage prohibitions creates a 'separateness' that betrays Judaism central commitment to the Oneness and awakening to. It also betrays the call for inner connectedness and guidance because a spiritual path cannot be enforced on anyone, not even by birth - it is one's Soul's calling. Being born into Judaism (or any religion) does not mean this is where one's Soul calling is. Even if one believes that one chooses the circumstance of their birth, there could be many reasons why one may have chosen to be born into a particular religion. We must each unveil the truth of our Soul and be true to it while also respect and 'love the stranger'.

Marriage is a sacred act taken by two adults who commit to share the journey of life with each other, support each other, and learn from each other while they each grow as human beings. Only the two people involved can decide whether they are physically, mentally, emotionally, and spiritually compatible to make this journey together. Each must listen within themselves. For some, sharing the exact same spiritual path with their partner is essential and they seek sameness. For others it is Ok to 'love the stranger' even if 'not be like the stranger,' they feel comfortable to 'invite' another religion in and find harmony with it. It may even connect them more with their own religion and allow the full kaleidoscope of core truths to unveil to them.

One's ability to stay true to ('distinguish from others') and pass on the religion of their birth is not subject to whether one marries a partner that shares this religion or not.

- It is first subject to them choosing the religion of their birth as their own. One can 'betray' the religion of their birth whether they marry a partner who shares it or not if this religion is not their calling and therefore not the religion of their choosing. Another religion may provide them with the way to connect and come Home and consequently, they may 'marry' into this religion.

- It is also subject to marrying a partner who respects their religion regardless of his/hers, own religion. A partner who appreciates the full kaleidoscope and is enriched by it, and who understands that one can 'love the stranger' even if not 'be like the stranger'.

Sharing a religion does not guarantee a successful union, for two people may differ in their spiritual aspirations even when they share the same religion.

Having two different religions does not invite marital discord, for two people with different religions may still share spiritual aspirations and although different, their religions can meet and create a beautiful harmony.

There is no right or wrong... It all depends on the individuals involved.

Living these realized truths may not be easy, particularly with loved ones and especially one's children. We desire and feel responsible to pass onto our children the religion we love and the connection we found through it to our Soul, to life, and the Source. Nevertheless, as in the words of Khalil Gibran "your children are not your children. They are the sons and daughters of life longing for itself".

When our children are young it is our responsibility to pass onto them the inner connection, the religion that guides us to this connection and its realized truths, and to stir them to journey safely and well… When they are adults, we must trust that we gave them the foundation and allow them to follow their Soul's calling as we must follow our own… We must remember there are many roads leading to Rome. While we can support and guide, we must not enforce, each must choose for themselves and take responsibility for their choices.

Holding on to cross-marriage prohibitions closes the door, suffocates the fire and the kaleidoscope of expressions; it contradicts the truth of Oneness, and therefore the truth of Judaism.

Forbidding cross-marriage is not peculiar to Judaism and the Jewish People, it is a prohibition shared by most other religions, races, and cultures. Nevertheless, since the Jewish People are committed to the truth of Oneness and to 'being a light unto the nation' - they must lead the way.

Treatment of non-Jew who wish to Covert to Judaism

Non-Jews who desire to join the 'Jewish Family' - by marriage or otherwise - can be met with relentless questioning from the 'Rabbinic Tribunal' and often be left feeling rejected and discouraged. This is true not only within Orthodox Judaism but also within certain schools of Traditional Judaism.

Some say this approach stems from 'loving the stranger' and 'not doing wrong by the stranger', and from recognizing the importance of 'non-enforcement'. Personal reflection is important to ensure one is fully aware of and is at peace with what they are committing themselves to. It is also important to ensure one's commitment is sincere and is fully their choice and not enforced on them.

While this is part of the truth, it is not all the truth... There is often is a lack of welcoming which projects an attitude of 'separateness' and perceived 'superiority'.

'Protecting' and 'not enforcing' to the point of discouragement, 'rejection' and 'exclusion' is not in line with Judaism's commitment to awakening to the truth of Oneness because the Oneness is always 'inclusive' not 'excluding'.

It also negates the promise to be 'a light unto the nations.' This requires us to allow the essence of Oneness to shine within and without for all to see and invite others to find same within themselves; it requires that when someone finds same within and expresses a desire to commit to it the Jewish way, we openly embrace them, not 'reject' them.

It is time to embrace and welcome the 'stranger' who knocks at our door...

What I am not allowed to do – you can do for me

There is the peculiar tendency by many observant Jews to engage non-Jews to attend to tasks that are not allowable to them. For example, an Orthodox Jew who observes a festive holy-day or the Shabbat may ask a non-Jew to press the lift button for him, or the crossing-light button, or the light switch etc. Similarly, Jews may engage non-Jews to push a baby pram for them as they walk to the synagogue or do any other task that they themselves will not do on a 'day of observance'.

This custom can be perceived as arrogant separateness and superiority for it is as if one says: 'I am not allowed to do so because it is not holy for me, but it is ok for you to do it for me'.

Some say this 'custom' is an expression of tolerance and freedom, a way of 'loving the stranger', of 'non-enforcing' and allowing others to hold to their beliefs and act as they choose. However, allowing someone to hold to their beliefs and to act as they choose is one thing, asking someone to do that which is not allowable to me and is considered wrongful by me is another – The first is an act of respect, the second an act of disrespect.

It is no different to asking someone to steal on one's behalf, or telling someone that they are not worthy enough and therefore they can engage in wrongful behaviours, or saying to someone: 'This is the underlying message in what I do, but you do not need worry about it, as a matter of fact, I need you not to worry about it because I need you to break my own belief of what is wrong for me to do by doing it for me'...

This behaviour is a contradiction and disrespectful approach that is out of alignment with being a 'light unto the nation' for one cannot 'model' one thing yet ask another to do the opposite, passing the message of "don't do as I do".

Whatever one's chosen practice is, it is not OK to ask another to do that which one considers wrong.

It is time for a respectful and loving attitude to our neighbour...

Conclusions

While Judaism and the Jewish People have shown in the past and still show tolerance and respect towards others and other religions, there are 'flaws' to attend to.

The 'diamond' of the commandments to find courage to 'distinguish from the stranger,' 'love the stranger,' and 'not do wrong by the stranger', are obscured by certain attitudes and behaviours that project 'separateness', 'intolerance' and 'superiority' and leave Judaism and the Jewish People wanting and compromised.

The Inter-relation between one Jew to Another

"Thou shalt love thy neighbour as thyself" (Levit. 19:18) is the commandment governing the way in which a Jew is to treat another Jew.

While this sentence has universal value, it was given to the Israelites at a time when there was no 'multiculturalism', when each 'culture'/ people lived in separate communities, and consequently, one's neighbour could only be of one's community. Therefore, it points to the way an Israelite (a Jew) is to treat another Israelite (another Jew).

Throughout history, Jewish communities supported and cared for individuals within them and supported and cared for each other's communities especially in times of difficulties. This attitude has supported the survival of the Jewish People through trials and tribulations.

This support does not promote undue internal protection. Alongside the instruction to 'love thy neighbour' one is also instructed: "thou shalt certainly rebuke thy neighbour, and not suffer sin on his account" (Levit. 19:17). One is required to stand by truth and good behaviour and never stand aside silently even if it means disclosing one's neighbour.

These guidelines offer a beautiful balance to follow...

Today, while care and support are still evident in Jewish and Israeli communities and while they strive to maintain internal integrity, one can also observe a division and loss of unity that can at times rise to alarming proportions.

In 1973, in a personal conversation with Richard Nixon, the US President, Golda Meir, then Prime Minister of Israel said: "You are the President of 150 million Americans; I am the Prime Minister of six million prime ministers." Israeli division is but a reflection of a wider tendency for Jewish division on a political, ethnic, ideological, and spiritual level.

This division – this kaleidoscope of expression - is not a problem, on the contrary, it is a healthy expression, for Judaism is:

A commitment to the journey of awakening the awareness to the fundamental truth of Oneness by means of individual inner connectedness and inner guidance.

Judaism encourages individual guidance and therefore individual expression.

The problem is the seemingly inability of the Jewish People to contain undue inner criticism and intolerance and to maintain a central unity in the face of the kaleidoscope of expression.

This inability is out of alignment with the truth of Oneness.

It results in unfortunate and destructive internal division that damages the diamond of "Thou shalt love thy neighbour as thyself".

It has led to much stumbling over the course of Jewish history from Biblical times to-date - Internal division led to the split between Israel and Judea, to the fall of both the first and second Temple, and it is now damaging Israeli society and Jewish communities around the world...

It is time to turn around, to be true to the Oneness and to the commitment to being a 'light unto the nations'... We can do so if we sincerely adhere to "Thou shalt love thy neighbour as thyself ".

The General behaviour of the Jewish People

The Jewish People are subjected to much criticism and stereotyping - both individually and collectively. Is this warranted?

The 'flaws' in the interactions with non-Jews and other religions and between Jews as pointed, bear some responsibility for this negative criticism and stereotyping. However, they can provide only a small justification for this dilemma. First, because despite all the issues raised, overall, the Jewish People behave honourably towards others and other religions, and with each other. Second, because historically, other religions have been (and still are) much more intolerant both without and within, yet they do not experience the same negative criticism and stereo typing.

Where does such criticism stem from? Can the cause be found in the way Jewish People and communities conduct themselves in the world?

Whether acknowledged or not, the individual and collective behaviour of the Jewish People is guided by their commitment to the truth of Oneness of Source and all life, and by the commandments and their underlying messages.

Jewish People and communities, both in Israel and in the world at large, foster a culture of behaviour that is honourable, self-sufficient, independent, and contributing, for they:

- Tend to work hard and be self-sufficient.
- Hold education and equal opportunity in high esteem and support it within their familial circles and communities.
- Even though they are a minority wherever they live (apart from in Israel) they are generally good citizens who respect their home country (be it Israel or otherwise) and seek to contribute and lead in however they can – be it in art, technology, medicine, science, economy, or the political and social arenas.

These values have allowed the Jewish People to survive and flourish both as individuals and as communities. These values have also allowed the State of Israel to be where it is today and to lead in many ways regardless of its mere turbulent 70 years of existence.

Unfortunately, these very values and contributions are often perceived as a desire for power and are subject to negative stereotyping rather than be recognized for what they are: A desire to excel, to contribute, to 'make the world a better place', to give and be one's best as well as be open to receive the best.

Nevertheless, alongside this generally honourable behaviour and contribution, there is at times 'undue crime, corruption, exploitation and abuse of power. These behaviours are not only self-defeating and destructive, but also out of alignment with the messages of the commandments and with Judaism' spirit of Oneness and the commitment to awaken to it. They provide a poor example and betray the commitment to be a light unto the nations.

These behaviours are not peculiar to the Jewish People and Communities. They manifest in all Communities and result from:

- A falling out of connection with Essence – The true light within, the Oneness within and without. For a Jewish person (or community), to lose connection with the Essence is not only a personal failure but also a 'Jewish failure' for the Essence is at the core of Judaism.
- They reflect a failed relationship with one's 'package deal.' One either fails to use the 'Package Deal[15]' as a stepping-stone to come Home and reconnect with one's Essence; or fails to use the 'Package Deal' in the light of an appropriate 'guiding compass'. For a Jewish person (or community) it is a failure to use the commandments as stepping-stones to reconnect, or to use them in the light of the 'guiding compass' of alignment with the truth of Oneness.

Although such behaviours in Jewish communities are generally lower than in other communities, they stir negative publicity and are used to justify the generalized negative stereotyping of Jewish People.

At the core lies an expectation that the Jewish People behave and act in the light of the highest moral stance. "What other individuals and/or nations may 'get away with', the Jewish People will be harshly criticized for!" (p48) ... This is the responsibility with which each individual Jew, and the Jewish People collectively,

---

[15]Referring to the 'package deal' of whichever religion one chose to align with.

were entrusted. Negative behaviours mark not only the individuals, but the whole Jewish community and indeed, the Spirit of Judaism itself.

It is vital for each individual Jew and each Jewish Community to take heart, reconnect and re-align...

Where to From Here

In the forthcoming chapters the following four themes will be explored:

- Relationship to God/ Source
- Marriage and gender relationships
- Dietary Laws
- Times and Seasons

These themes with their related commandments hold a central part in Judaism and form the basis to many of today's practices and to the behaviour of Jewish People and communities around the world.

Chapter 12:
Relationship to The Source of Life (God)

The commandments and practices in this theme are central and upon them all else is founded for they point not only to one's relationship with the Source of Life[16] but also to one's relationship with one's Soul.

Judaism is founded on the realization that we and all that exists, emanate from One Source (the God Without), and each individual existence is a flame of this Source. This flame is the Soul, or Inner Source, or the God Within (refer to inner journey pp 8-15). Therefore, our relationship with the One Source is inevitably, a reflection of our relationship with our Soul and vice versa.

In the language and culture of its time these commandments aim to ensure we remember where we have come from and establish a respectful and reverent relationship with the One Source; and that we remember who we truly are and establish a respectful and reverent relationship with ourselves - with our Soul.

---

[16]The Source of Life = God or whatever one's perception of the source of life, be it the Life-Force, Universal-Energy, 'Nature', or whatever else...

All else stems from these relationships...

The Central Commandments
The relationship with The One Source and our Soul

The basis for any relationship is an acknowledgement of existence and a willingness to stay true to it.

In the language and culture of the time we are commanded to:

1. Acknowledge the existence of the Source of life (Ex. 20:2; Deut. 5:6).
2. Remember its Oneness, Unity, Wholeness and Eternity (Deut. 6:4).
3. Not foster doubts regarding its existence and Oneness to set in (Ex.20:3).

Without these conditions there cannot be a relationship with the Source of Life and with our Soul, and there cannot be a commitment to stay true to the ongoing journey of awakening to the truth of One Source.

These are the messages of these commandments.

We are also told to fully love the One Source (Deut. 6:5) and treat its 'name' with reverence (Ex. 22:28; Lev. 22:32 and 24:16).

This is not about satisfying God's ego but realizing that any healthy relationship, including our relationship with the One Source and our Soul, must be founded on love. Only then can we be in the relationship and live freely, peacefully, joyfully, and openly.

In contradiction, we are commanded to fear the One Source, and inevitably fear our own Soul. One is warned that any 'blasphemy' is to be punished by death. (Deut. 6:13 & 10:20 and Lev 24:16).

How can one love and fear at the same time? How can a relationship based on fear be respectful, loving, nurturing and supportive?

Where is the love and wisdom in penalizing one's stumbling with death?

Using Oneness as a 'guiding compass' we realize that if taken literally, these commandments are out of alignment. We must look beyond the words to their underlying meaning as per the language and terminology of the time.

Doing so unveils that:

1. The term 'fearing' was often used to express 'great reverence and awe' rather than actual fear.

2. Unlike the culture of Moses and the Israelites, most cultures of the time were founded on fearing God (the Source), on 'blind obedience' to God, and perceiving God to be separate from man and from life. Shifting from such a culture to a culture of love, of discipline couple with reflection, and of Oneness - a recognition that all life is a flame of God, may have felt too threatening to the non-Israelites and maybe even to the Israelites who lived under the culture of fear, 'blind obedience', and separateness during their 400years of enslavement. Moses (or the writer of the commandment) may have used the terminology of 'to fear reverently' as a way of closing the gap between fear and love, and between separateness and Oneness, to bring all into covenant.

3. A failure to love the Source of Life and its flame within us - our Soul - results in 'spiritual death' and depression. Using the language of the time 'punishment by death' may have been the best way for Moses (or the writer) to pass on this message. If we were to use today's language and terminology, we would say that a healthy self-love is at the essence of living freely and happily and having loving relationships. Much of the depression suffered these days by far too many, results from a lack of healthy self-love and from a failing relationship with oneself and the Source Within (the God Within) and the Source Without (the God Without).

It is also possible that the language of fear and of punishment by death was not written by Moses himself but added later, most likely by the Priests, as a reflection of the culture of fear or for the purpose of retaining power through fear, hence rendering these elements obsolete.

One can see how the 'guiding Compass' of Oneness and the context of time can shed light on the commandments and allows for their shining diamond to unveil.

The relationship with the Torah and its Commandments

We are commanded to:

- Revere the Torah, study it and its commandments and teach it (Deut. 6:7).
- Write it ourselves (Deut. 31:9).
- Neither to add to nor detract from the commandments (Deut. 13:1).

Reverence to the Torah and its commandments unites the Jewish People. This is not surprising, for when seen through the 'guiding compass' of alignment with the truth of Oneness and the context of time, language, culture and purpose, the Torah and its commandments hold universal wisdom.

Only by leaving the words as they are – neither adding to them nor detracting from them - will it be possible at any point of time to see them in the light of the language, culture, and purpose of their time, and understand their true meaning, purpose, and message, so it can be carried into the future as life and humans evolve.

As for Torah study, there is much wisdom in the message to make it part of one's life. It ensures the Torah is kept alive and stays a living part of one's life. However, some sectors of Judaism – mostly strict Orthodox Jewish communities, and especially in Israel - make Torah studying the sole purpose of one's life.

While one is free to choose to make Torah study their life purpose if this is their Soul's calling and gift -

1. One cannot and should not enforce it on others.
    In many Orthodox communities, Torah study is the only 'permissible life-style.' Children are often sent to schools where they learn mostly Torah and their potential is limited. Everything that is not Torah, be it science, art, music etc is often prohibited. It is a path that does not allow, and even forbids, the 'climber' to see the view as he aims for the top of the mountain. One is free to choose such for oneself, but should not enforce same on others, yet it often is

enforced within Orthodox communities and at times there is an attempt to enforce it outside the community, on more secular communities.

2. One cannot expect others to carry and sustain them and their choices. In some strict Orthodox communities (specifically in Israel) where Torah study is the only 'permissible life- style', they also choose not to work or perform civil duties. They expect the State and its serving citizens to sustain and support them and their families.

There are Orthodox communities where although they focus on Torah studies, they also allow children to express themselves in other ways, where members work and are self-sufficient and contributing citizens. But this is not the case in many other Orthodox communities. These behaviours not only obscure the beauty of 'studying the Torah', but also cause destructive community division.

It is time to allow the true diamond of Torah study to shine...

Central Practices within The Theme

The Israelites were given symbolic practices acting as constant reminders of the covenant and the commitment to the ongoing journey of awakening to the Oneness to ensure that we do not forget the truths of One Source, of where we have come from, and who we are - in other words that we remember our Soul and its Source.

They also aim to bring this covenant, commitment, and truths into everyday living.

These symbolic practices include -

1. The circumcision of every male child on his eight day of life (Gen. 17:12 and Lev. 12:3) - It is a reminder by mean of marking the body, the only symbolic act given by Abraham.
2. The marking of men's corners of clothing by wearing Tzizit (Num.15:38) - A mark on one's clothes to be seen during the day so one constantly remembers.
3. The marking of all doorposts without and within one's home by fixing on them a condensed script of the Torah (mezuza) (Deut.6:9) – This acts as a reminder each time one enters and exits one's home and as one moves within the home.
4. For men to bind Tefillin (a condensed script of the Torah) to the head and arm everyday (Deut. 6:8) - Ensuring one remembers at the beginning of each day.
5. Reciting the prayer of Shema each morning on waking and each night before sleeping (Deut. 6:7) – Once more, it ensures one remembers at the beginning and the end of each day.
6. Saying Grace before and after each meal (Deut. 8:10) - An expression of gratitude and appreciation for nourishing the body.

It is easy to get lost in everyday living. The underlying message of all these commanded practices is clear:

Engage in symbolic acts that engage your body, home, words, heart, and your mind every day, to constantly remember who you are – your Soul, the Source Within - and where you come from - the Source of all Life. Remember the Oneness of the Source of

Life and the commitment to stay on the journey of awakening to it and living by it.

These symbolic acts are all a means to an end, not an end of itself, it is their underlying messages that are the essence. They were all prescribed in the context of a certain time and culture, and while it maybe one's soul calling to use them all, and use them as prescribed, others may feel aligned with only some of these symbolic acts, or may feel called to live these messages using different symbolic acts which better serve them to remember and express the commitment.

If we forget the message and focus on the prescribed symbolic practices making them an end unto themselves, and if we forget to factor in the context of time and culture, these symbolic practices can become a source of internal intolerance and division whereby:

Jews who use them, or use them as prescribed, can harshly judge Jews who do not use them or use them differently.

Jews who do not use them or use them differently may scoff at Jews who use them or use them as prescribed.

Consequently, the beauty of the truth of Oneness that they are meant to express and protect is lost.

To a greater or lesser extent, this intolerance and division is a reality within today's Judaism... It is time to clear this up and to allow the diamond of these beautiful messages to shine.

Chapter 13:
Family, Marriage and Gender Relationships

Judaism values and respects inter-human relationships not only with non-Jews and other Jews, but also within families – between parents and children and husband and wife - and sexual interactions. There are about 54 commandments covering these matters which are the foundation to Judaism's attitude to family, women & men generally, women-men inter-relations, and sexuality.

Parent-child relationship

Respect from children to parents holds an important place in Jewish families.

While one is not commanded to love one's father and/or mother, one is commanded to honour and revere them and not smite nor curse them.

Father and mother hold equal place within these commandments as Judaism equally respects males and females within the family unit.

One wonders at some patriarchal attitudes within Judaism in general and some sections of Orthodox Judaism in particular, where education and life opportunities afforded to women are far inferior to what is offered to its men. All too often women's primary role and purpose is to be wives and mothers and 'a procreation vessel'. While it is perfectly OK for any woman to choose this if this is her calling, it is not OK to 'enforce' any woman into this role if her calling differs.

Patriarchal attitudes are not peculiar to Judaism, but they are not at Judaism's foundation nor are they aligned with Judaism's core truth of Oneness of Source and all Life.

(Ref: Ex. 20:12; 21:15; 21:17 & Lev. 19:3)

Attitude to Children

Judaism is founded on the sanctification and approval of life, humanity, and all living beings, and on the recognition of the essential goodness of all life, of humanity, and all living beings. This is expressed in Genesis first through the blessing that concludes each day of creation/ evolution: "And God saw that it was good" (Genesis 1;10/12/13/14); and second, through the specific blessing given to humanity to "be fruitful and multiply" (Gen. 1:28).

These sanctifications, recognitions and approvals are a natural result of the Oneness of all life.

In Judaism, children are seen as a blessing.

In many Orthodox Jewish communities, the approval of life and humanity, and the welcoming of children is perceived as a commandment to have as many children as possible. In these communities, women birth one child after another often having 10 or more children. While there is nothing wrong with this perception of itself or with a choice to have as many children as one wishes, it is important to –

- Recognize this practice for what it is: a chosen interpretation
- Ensure it is the woman's free choice, and/or her Soul calling and not something 'expected of her' or 'enforced on her'.

However, in many strict Orthodox communities, this 'translation' is regarded as a 'non-negotiable' commandment to have an abundance of children and therefore it is a demanded and expected lifestyle. For many women within such strict communities this non-negotiable expectation is at the cost of their right to choose for themselves, and the cost of their well-being (be it physical, mental, emotional, or even spiritual).

Also, while some Orthodox families may have the financial capacity to cater for an expanding family, in many other Orthodox families this is not the case. The father who is supposed to be the bread winner, is often fully engaged in Torah study from a young age and chooses to continue this into adulthood; he has little earning capacities and there is an expectation that the State's Government welfare system carries the welfare costs for his ongoing expanding family.

This situation must be faced as the result is:

- Gender discrimination and inequality of rights and opportunities for women,
- Mental and physical health issues for some women,
- Economic burden and social discord and division.

Attitude to Women throughout Marriage

While Judaism is seen to be patriarchal, when held in the context of their time, most of the commandments regarding the treatment of women, particularly in marriage, protect women from abuse and inappropriate sexual or other exploitation, and ensure respect, care, and a responsible approach from a man to a woman and in particular, from a husband to wife.

This is clearly expressed in the following commandments:

- Men are not to have intimate relations with a woman unless they commit to honour her by the sacrament of marriage. (Deut. 23:18 & 24:1)
- A man who attempts to seduce a woman is to pay a penalty. (Ex. 22:15)
- In the case of a rape, a man must marry his victim, care for her and is never allowed to divorce her. (Deut. 22:28-29)
- In a marriage, a husband is forbidden to withhold food, clothing, and conjugal rights from his wife. (Ex. 21:10)
  This commandment states not only Judaism's protection of women but also approval, respect, and ease with all human needs including physical and sexual needs. This ease is further expressed through the commandment that a newly married husband must be free to attend to his wife for the first year and be exempt from taking any form of public labour – be it military service or similar. (Deut. 24:5)
- Women are protected from false accusations by their husband and if a husband defames his wife's honour through evil reports of unchastity, he is commanded to care for her for his lifetime. (Deut. 22:19)

- Women are also protected in the event of divorce. Judaism does not forbid divorce but demands that it be done by a formal written document. A woman can re-marry following a divorce and an ex-husband cannot demand that she re-marries him. (Deut. 24:1 & 4)
- A woman who becomes a widow and is childless, is protected by a commandment stating that her husband's brother must marry her unless she formally releases him from this obligation. (Deut. 25:5 & 7-9)

These commandments may seem absurd in today's world, but when seen in the context of the time they were given they reflect respectful and protective treatment of women.

Nevertheless, patriarchal attitudes still exist in Jewish Communities. The stricter an Orthodox community is, the more this patriarchal attitude seems to be. They manifest through the limitations placed on women's rights for education and opportunities and their roles within their communities. This impacts on their right to fulfil themselves in roles that are outside the wife-mother role expected of them.

There are many customs that subdue women where the origin remains a mystery. Most are practiced within Orthodox communities such as:

Covering the head, wearing a wig after marriage, and dressing where no part of the body is 'visible' (long sleeves, high neck tops, long skirts etc).

None of these have any origin in Judaism. It is OK if a woman chooses this 'style' for herself and is fully aware of the reason and purpose of such customs, however, they are a poor choice if imposed on her as 'tradition'.

Other customs - such as the woman circling the man seven times at the wedding ceremony, implying that from now on he is the centre of her life - are a clear expression of inequality, for the groom is not expected to reciprocate same... Surprisingly, many independently minded young brides choose to follow this custom and while they are totally free to do so one wonders if they are aware of its significance.

It may be time to explore all this if we are to allow the true diamond of Judaism's intended message of respect and equality to shine, and if we are to act as a 'model' for others.

Allowed and Forbidden Sexual Relationships

Judaism is generally at ease with physical intimacy which is perceived as a right for both man and woman. Judaism perceives Nazariteship (being a Monk) as an 'un-natural' state and a man can commit to such for only a limited time (Num. 6:3-9). There is however an expectation that sexual behaviour is honourable, and there are commandments that indicate clearly what is OK and what is not.

All sexual relationships are strictly between humans only and any intercourse with a beast is strictly forbidden to both man and woman. (Refer to Lev. 18:23)

All incestual relationships are forbidden. These include sexual interactions with:

A parent - be it mother, father, or even stepmother/stepfather

A child - be it minor or adult, be it one's biological child or one's child by marriage.

A sibling – be it blood sibling, sibling by a parent second marriage, or sibling- in-law (that is, wife of a brother or brother of a wife etc.).

A grandparent - be it biological or non-biological grandparents.

A grandchild – be it biological or non-biological grandchildren.

An uncle/aunt – be it biological or uncles/aunt by marriage.

A nephew/niece – be it biological or by marriage.

(Refer to Lev. 18:7; 18:8, 18:9, 18:10-18)

So strict were these commandments in relation to incest that fearful of any temptation, physical contact between relatives including kissing, embracing, winking etc was forbidden lest it leads to incest (Lev. 18:6). Unfortunately, with such prohibition, innocence was taken out of natural non-sexual expressions of affection, and all contacts were unintentionally sexualized. This commandment must be seen in the context of its time – a time when incestual relationships were prominent and the only way to uproot them was to deny all contact. Many Orthodox communities still practice such prohibitions, and it may be time to de-sexualize human contact, restore innocence, and the ability to express non-sexual physical affection in our human relationships.

All sodomy is forbidden - Man with man sexual relationships including incestual man-man sexual relationships such as father and son, and nephew and uncle. Interestingly woman-woman relationship does not seem to be regarded as sodomy and is not forbidden. (Refer to Lev 18:7; 14 & 22)

There is also prohibition on all transgender behaviour. Not only is a man not to wear woman's clothing and a woman is not to wear man's cloths, changing one's gender of birth is unthinkable. (Deut. 22:5)

Today, while incestual relationships remain forbidden, there is a growing understanding and respect for human biological-sexual diversity and needs. Progressive Judaism alongside other progressive movements for sexual liberation accepts the kaleidoscope of human sexual expressions and recognizes that human love has many faces. Sexual relationships between two consenting men or two consenting women are not seen as sinful nor forbidden. Likewise, transgender behaviour is better understood.

This is not the case in more conservative Judaism and in most Orthodox Judaism communities where gay/ lesbian relationships, and transgender behaviour remain sinful and are forbidden.

It is time to look at these commandments in the context of their time and move towards respect and appreciation for all life and expression.

If human sexual behaviour is to be preserved with integrity and respect, it must always be between two consenting adults – This message is made clear throughout all the commandments and is the condition to honourable man-woman intimacy. While human sexual intimacy needs and rights are honoured, they are subject to free choice on both sides, and offer extra protection to women by prohibiting men to:

- Unduly seduce or enforce such a relationship on a woman.
- Have intercourse with another man's wife.
- Have intercourse with a woman during her menstrual periods.

(Refer to Deut. 22:28-29 & 23:18, Ex. 22:15, Lev. 18:20)

Indeed today, apart from when it comes to incestual relationships, free consent between two adults should be the most important criterion so that human sexual behaviour can be preserved with integrity and respect. It is time for Judaism and the Jewish People to lead the way by taking this message to the world...

Chapter 14:
Dietary Laws

The Dietary Laws contain roughly 50 commandments. They include 'Kashrut laws' - allowable and non-allowable foods be they plant-based (fruits, vegetables, grains etc) or animal-based (dairy, eggs and meat), Agricultural practices and Animal Husbandry, and one's relationship with and attitude to food, the earth and animals.

The dietary commandments reflect biological and spiritual understanding and recognize the interconnectedness and oneness of Body and Soul. They convey messages of humility, respect, kindness, and gratitude, and tell us that what we eat, how we relate to the food we eat, and how we treat the source of the food we eat – matters.

The Commandments and their related practices

Attitudes to Food

We are commanded to –

- Rejoice in the food we eat, and treat it as a blessing.
- Eat respectfully and not like a glutton or drunkard.

- Bless the food we eat before eating, and express gratitude for it by saying Grace after each meal.
  (Refer to Ex. 23:25, Deut. 12:7, Lev. 19:26, Deut. 21:20 and Deut. 8:10)

Agricultural Practices and allowable and non-allowable plant-based foods

While all plant food is allowable, there are laws addressing the treatment of plant food and its source - the earth. They reflect not only agricultural knowledge but also care for all life.

1. Farmers are commanded not to mix plant species and not to plant a mix of trees, seeds, and herbs in the same field. It is a message of both well-being and respect for the earth.
   Different grains, seeds, and fruit trees have differing agricultural needs, and a mixed field can deplete the soil resulting in products unsuitable for human consumption. (Refer to Lev. 19:19, Deut. 22:9)
2. Farmers are also commanded not to eat the fruit of a tree for the first three years after planting. A tree takes three years to fully mature and for its fruit to be fit for consumption. Additionally, on the fourth year, the fruit is regarded as sacred and is to be either donated or eaten in community as an expression of appreciation and gratitude. (Refer to Lev. 19:23-24)
3. There are lessons of social care and justice which ensure one does not become greedy or disregard the less fortunate.
   Farmers are commanded to leave ungathered a portion of their fields for the poor and unfortunate. While gathering,

they are also commanded to leave any produce that has fallen to the ground for the poor.
(Refer to Lev. 19:9-10 & 23:22, Deut. 24:19-21).

4. The source of all plant food – the earth – must not be exploited, it needs time to 'rest' and rejuvenate. Farmers are commanded to allow a Sabbatical year every seventh year - a year in which the earth is to lie fallow and not be tilled.

    The Sabbatical year reinforces social justice and respect for all life, for any crop/ fruit that grows during the Sabbatical year is to be left untouched for the poor, the less fortunate, and for wildlife to enjoy.
    (Refer to Ex. 23:10-11, Lev. 25:2-7 & 20-22, Deut. 15:1-3).

Animal Husbandry Practices and allowable and non-allowable animal-based foods'

The bulk of the commandments under the 'Dietary Laws' relate to animal husbandry and animal-based food (dairy, eggs, and meat).

This is not surprising because Judaism is founded on the realization of Oneness of Source and life. It recognizes that living requires us to sustain our body however, when we choose to consume animal-based foods or animals' products such as wool, eggs etc we disconnect from the ultimate being of the other and are out of alignment with the Oneness. The commandments regarding Animal Husbandry and allowable and non-allowable animal-based foods aim to raise human awareness and to ensure that we preserve, as much as possible, our Soul's love and integrity, treat animals with utmost compassion and respect and protect them from undue suffering, as well as protect our biological well-being.

General Animal Husbandry

Kindness, respect, and care for animals is central to these commandments. They forbid one to:

- Overload a working beast or leave it unaided if it has fallen beneath its burden.
- Yoke together two beasts of different species, as different animals have different abilities and unlawful joining can overburden them and cause undue suffering, especially to the weaker animal.
- Overwork an animal. One's working animals and herd must be allowed to rest and rejuvenate on Shabbat and on all the holy-days and festivals.
- Crossbreed cattle (or birds) of different species is abusive as it can cause illness, deformity, and discomfort.
  (Refer to Deut. 22:4; Ex. 20:10, 23:5, 23:12 & 34:21; Lev. 19:19)

Allowable and non-allowable animal-based food

Human physical and spiritual well-being is central of these commandments. They clearly state the animals allowable for human consumption and the ones that are not.

Allowable animals include:

- Land animals with split hooves that chew their cud - cows, goats, sheep, and deer.
  All other land animals - dogs, cats, rodents, rabbits, pigs, horses, snakes, and land insects - are not allowed.
- Water animals with fins and scales which include most fish but exclude reptiles, shellfish, dolphins, seals, and whales
- Birds are limited to chicken, turkey, duck, and pheasant.

All other birds - birds of prey, scavengers, vultures, and flying insects - are not allowed.

The common thread is that all animals allowable for human consumption are herbivores who feed on plants and seeds (although not all herbivores are allowed). All carnivores - animals which feed on other animals- scavengers, and animals feeding on secretion - are not.

These restrictions reflect care for body and soul:

- The health of the body – Plant food (as we will later come to see) is the natural food to sustain the human body, which is why only plant eating animals are deemed fit for human consumption. Eating animals which feed on other animals, are scavengers, or feed on secretion, risks our physical well-being.
- The health of the Soul (spiritual health) – When we consume carnivores, scavengers, animals who feed on secretion or non-allowable herbivore, we foster an unhealthy attitude of indiscriminate consumption. Consuming carnivores fosters 'chain killing'. These lack reverence for life and are disrespectful to us and another being - They are out of alignment with the truth of Oneness. When we are out of alignment with the truth of Oneness we are out of alignment with our Soul. Being out of alignment with our Soul risks our spiritual well-being.

These messages are enforced by further limitations on the consumption of 'allowable animals':

1. One is not to eat an allowable animal if found dead in the fields. This protects the body -for one does not know how

the animal died – and the Soul – by showing respect, reverence, and compassion to a life of another that has suffered enough.
(Refer to Ex. 22:30; Deut. 14:21).

2. Not all parts of the allowable animals are permitted. Non-allowable body parts are the nerves, veins, tallow-fats, and the blood as they can contain bacteria, parasites, pathogens, and heme iron, which can pose a health risk. From a spiritual perspective - blood is life and while we may eat the flesh, we cannot and must not 'consume' its life – its spirit...
(Refer to Lev. 11:2, 4, 9, 11, 13, 21, 41-44, & 46; Lev. 17:13-14; Deut.14:11 & 19; Gen. 32:33; Lev. 7:23 & 26).

Treatment of animals allowable for human consumption

Protecting animals from undue suffering and ensuring a respectful and compassionate approach is the focus of these commandments. They include-

- 'Lawful' ways to slaughter an animal to minimize (as much as possible) pain and stress.
- A prohibition on slaughtering an animal and its young on the same day. This also applies to a mother-bird and its young.
- Setting a mother bird free if her nest was taken.
- A prohibition to cook the young in its mother's milk.
(Det. 12:21-23 & 22:6-7; Lev 22:28; Ex. 23:19 & 34:26)

The 'Mud' that obscures the 'Diamond' of These Commandments

The environmental, biological, and spiritual wisdom, and the respect, compassion, and reverence to all life, emanating from the 'Dietary Laws' are their shining 'diamond'.

Many commandments relating to the treatment of agricultural land are still practiced in Israel and on kosher farms today, including the care of the needy. However, when it comes to Animal Husbandry and the treatment of animals it differs. Some commandments are practiced today (such as - allowable and non-allowable animal-based foods and kosher slaughtering) however, they are often practiced in ways that are out of context with the Spirit in which they were intended, and which neglect their deeper messages.

This calamity results from failing to see these commandments in the light of –

- Their alignment with the Compass of Oneness (alignment with the truth of Oneness).
- The context of the culture of the time.

If we are to sincerely adhere to the spirit of the given commandments and to their intended messages, stay true to the truth of Oneness and to being 'a light unto the nations', we must be willing to acknowledge this calamity, and most importantly - attend to it!

Cross Breeding

Outlawing cross breeding aims to prevent animal abuse and undue suffering of illness, deformity, and discomfort.

We may not see cross breeding between cattle species (i.e. camel and cow), or between bird species (i.e. chicken and turkey), however, much cross breeding is done with the sole purpose of serving human interest:

- Cattle and birds[17] that grow faster – to enable earlier slaughter,
- Cattle and birds that grow 'fatter' to give us 'more meat',
- Cattle and sheep that give us more milk,
- Sheep that give us more wool,
- Birds that give us more eggs.

To mention but a few...

These forms of cross breeding were not specified in the commandments because they did not exist at the time the commandments were given - the knowledge required to practice them was not available. They cause as much misery, suffering and discomfort to the animals as the forms of cross breeding that were specifically forbidden, and they portray the same attitude that the lives of animals hold no value except to serve our human need and greed.

These practices are sad and unethical enough when practiced within the animal agriculture industry around the world, they are devastating when practiced in farms in Israel and other animal farms deemed 'kosher'.

There is nothing 'kosher' about inflicting suffering on animals. They are hollow practices abiding by words devoid of their intended meaning and message, they are out of alignment with the commitment to awaken to the truth of Oneness, out of alignment with the reverence to all life... out of alignment with Judaism...

---

[17] I do not mention pigs and other animals consumed by humans only because they are not deemed allowable. However non-allowable animals are inflicted with the same suffering.

'Kosher' Slaughtering

The commandments regarding kosher slaughtering were given at a time when animals were killed in whatever way and with whatever 'tools' one had. The best one could do to protect the animals was installing laws for 'proper slaughtering' to minimize - as much as possible - the animal's suffering in its last moments of life.

What we see today is a rigid adherence to practices that may have been the best available thousands of years ago, without considering there may be more compassionate options available today. Once again, the intended message of compassion, care and reverence for life is lost to rigid adherence to a bygone practice.

Sadder still is the fact that nothing much seems to have been learnt in thousands of years of human evolution and the evolution of Judaism and Jewish People...

There is a school of Rabbis who believe that apart from minimizing animals' suffering, the law of 'Schita' ('proper kosher slaughtering') was intended to take compassion and respect for animals' life a step further... They aimed to bring to human's awareness the animals' suffering and distress, and to support the realization that one is taking the life of a living, breathing, and feeling being. Rejecting causing such pain, the consumption of meat would be all together abandoned. As Sir Paul McCartney said in acknowledgement of the unimaginable suffering animals endure in today's factory farms and slaughterhouses: "If slaughterhouses had glass walls, everyone would be vegetarian".

But the slaughterhouses walls are made of brick not of glass and the world still refuses to see. Worse, the Jewish People refuse to see and have not moved forward in their journey of awakening to the truth of Oneness – for if they had, they could not turn away... Consequently, the 'diamond' of this commandment with its intended message is obscured by 'mud', as is the Jewish People commitment to move towards the Oneness and to be 'a light unto the nations'.

Separating Milk from Meat

A central practice in Judaism's dietary regime is the separation of Milk from Meat.

While the more strictly Orthodox a household is, the more strictly this is adhered to, it is practiced to a greater or lesser extent in most Jewish homes. Some homes may have either a milk or a meat centred meal. Other homes take it further with different plates, utensils, pots, and pans etc for milk and meat-based products and meals. Some homes take it further still with separate stoves, sinks and dishwashers.

The source of this practice is the commandment "Thou shall not boil a kid in its mother's milk"; a commandment deemed important enough to be repeated twice (Ex. 23:19 & Ex. 34:26). Because it was repeated twice some Rabbis believed it intended to send two messages regarding the treatment of animals.

The first message is that it is forbidden to remove a suckling-young from its mother. It is a clear message of minimal compassionate treatment and respect for animals' life, telling us that –

- The young animal belongs with its mother.
- Separating mother and child while the young is dependent on its mother is cruel and causes undue suffering to the young and the mother.

- Taking the young while it is suckling so we can satisfy our desire for tender meat, or benefit from the mother's milk is cruel and the utmost disregard for animal life.
- The basic right of every animal is to reach maturity before being used for human purpose.

The same moral code for compassionate treatment for animals is also in the commandments not to slaughter any animal/bird and its young on the same day and to set a mother bird free if one takes her nest. (Det. 12:21-23 & 22:6-7; Lev 22:28). It stems naturally from the truth of Oneness and the reverence for all life - The truth upon which Judaism is founded.

The second message enforces compassionate treatment and respect for animals' life from a different perspective. It forbids 'cooking' a cow/bull in the milk of the mother cow.

This is not a health issue (as some claim) but an ethical issue. The practice of separating milk from meat grew from this aspect of the commandment, to ensure that an 'off-spring' would never be cooked in the milk of its mother.

Following this practice - as far as one wishes - is a compassionate expression. It becomes a problem only when –

- The practice is not seen for what it is: Compassion and respect for animal life.
- One does not recognize that there are many ways to express this compassion - having separate dishes or two kitchens is OK if one chooses, but it is not the only way, nor a necessity.
- One judges others, deeming their home 'not kosher' if they choose to practice this moral message differently (such as

washing their utensils rather than having separate sets), or even if they feel the possibility is so remote that the meat they eat is an 'off-spring' of the dairy they use, that such separation is unnecessary.

But worse, it is a problem when –

- All that remains of this beautiful commandment is the mere practice of separating milk products from meat products, while its deep moral message is lost... For while we may no longer yolk together animals of different species the treatment of animals in farms leaves much to be desired...

In many Jewish homes, where separating milk from meat is fastidiously adhered to –

- The meat that is separated from the milk comes from factory farms where cattle and birds are cross bred to produce fast growth and 'fatter' stock, where their life is short and miserable and leads to an even more gruesome death. Yet it gets the 'kosher' stamp...
- The milk that is separated from the meat comes from dairies where cows are artificially and forcibly inseminated year after year. The calves are taken away from the mothers immediately or short after birth and their milk is stolen to serve humans. Dairy farmers report hearing the mothers bellow for their young days, even weeks after such cruel separation... When the cows are spent and can no longer birth or produce milk, they meet a gruesome end at the slaughterhouse... If their calves are females, they are raised by human hands as quickly as possible so they too start the same miserable life cycle as their mothers; if they are males,

they are treated as 'unwanted excess' and are either left to die or taken straight to the slaughterhouse to satisfy the human desire for the tender meat of the young (veal)... Yet it gets the 'kosher' stamp...

In these same kitchens where meat and milk are strictly separated, the chickens and the eggs come from farms where - with very few exceptions - hens and chicks experience nothing but torturous lives...

They are bred for fast growth and to produce as many eggs as possible.

They are locked in cages, or in cramped barns - only very few 'lucky ones' may occasionally get to feel the sun, grass and the air.

They are nothing but egg producing machines and when their bodies are spent, they meet the same gruesome death as the cows.

If used for breeding they will produce endless fertilised eggs but never get to nurture their young... And once they are spent, they are slaughtered.

The fertilized eggs are incubated till hatched; male chicks, just like male calves, are treated as 'excess' to be disposed of shortly after hatching – shredded alive in machines like they were nothing but lifeless paper... Female chicks are fed and fattened to follow their mother's fate and be either egg producing machines or breeding machines till their bodies are exhausted and they too are sent to slaughter.

Yet, this too gets the 'kosher' stamp...

I was dismayed to learn that while caged and barn laid eggs may be 'not morally OK', they are not against 'Halacha' (Jewish interpreted law). Does this not render Halacha not kosher and invalid? - For it is out of alignment with the very foundation of Judaism and with its commitment to awakening to the Oneness and to the reverence for all life.

It is bad enough when these atrocities happen in factory farming across the world, but for them to also be practiced in Israel and in farms that are deemed as kosher - it is unimaginable... Kosher is not always kosher...

Separating milk from meat has sadly become a hollow practice that lost its soul... but no one seems to notice or care as long as the practice is carried on.

My intention is to reveal and bring to light the 'mud' obscuring the 'diamond' of Judaism's compassion and reverence to all life. To point that this 'mud' results from -

- Focusing on a practice while forgetting its intended message and purpose.
- Allowing an interpretation to become the truth while the truth is forgotten.
- Not using the 'guiding compass' of the truth of Oneness - for when a practice is out of alignment with the truth of Oneness, it is out of alignment with Judaism.

It is time to be true and awaken to the truth of Oneness...

Relating to Other life and Eating 'flesh'

The greatest failure of all is the inevitable betrayal of the ongoing journey of awakening to the truth of Oneness - the very core and foundation of Judaism.

Humans were blessed and given mastery and dominion over the earth and all living things that creep the earth, the sea and its fish life, and the sky with its birds' life. (Genesis 1:28). Unfortunately, with this blessing came the man-made notion that humans have the right to do as they please with the planet, and other life forms, and that all life exists for human benefit. Nothing could be further from the truth. 'Dominion' is always about care, responsibility, and compassion, never about privilege, right, misuse of power, or abuse.

A king may have 'dominion' over his subjects, this always means he has the responsibility to care for his subjects. If he abuses his subjects for his own benefit, he becomes a totalitarian dictator. An abusive 'dominion' reflects a non-contextual reading of human position on the planet, and most certainly a non-contextual reading of Judaism which is founded on the realization of Oneness and a commitment to awaken one's awareness to it.

This distorted notion of 'dominion', and the necessity of treating all life with reverence, reveals when one follows the blessing to its conclusion.

Following the blessing, mankind was told: "See, I give you every seed-bearing plant that is upon all the earth, and every tree that has seed-bearing fruit; they shall be yours for food" (Genesis 1:28-29).

Animals were never meant to be for our physical nourishment. A plant-based diet is not only the natural, healthy, and ethical way of eating, it is also the only way of eating that is aligned with the truth of Oneness of Source and all life, and therefore it is Judaism at its core...

It is not only these primary words in Genesis that express this truth, ponder these:

- Animals are not a magical reservoir of calcium, protein & iron. They get everything they need from plants and so do we! The commandments pass on this message by telling us that, should we develop a desire for meat, only plant feeding animals are 'acceptable' for human consumption – for we too are meant to eat a plant-based diet.
- Unlike carnivores our body does not have the flexibility to stalk, jump and run after prey... We do not have claws to grab and hold prey... We do not have teeth capable of killing prey in mere seconds... We do not have the instinct or skill to hunt that are seen in hunting-animal from an early age... We have had to invent tools to enable us to hunt, and have had to learn the skills to hunt... Human desire for meat is acquired not innate.

Humanity has become lost and has moved from a world of Oneness and reverence for all life, to a world of duality and separateness. A world where humans have become separated from the planet and other living beings; where they perceive themselves to be superior and 'allow' themselves to consume and use for their benefit whatever walks, crawls, flies, or swim.

It is traditionally held that the 'big flood' in Noach's time resulted from humanity's failure and the loss of Oneness. Yet, the floods did nothing to support the 'restoration of Oneness'...

Following the flood, possibly due to the environmental damage and the shortage of plant-based foods, humans succumbing to their needs and desire, 'gave themselves permission' to consume flesh. Unfortunately, with this 'permission', the duality[18] became anchored, and the lost Oneness, not only was not restored, it deepened and grew into abusive 'dominion'.

One wonders whether carnivores – meat eating animals – also evolved from this time of the floods because Genesis equally specifies: "And to every beast of the earth, and to every bird of the air, and to everything that creeps on the earth, wherein there is life, I have given every green herb for food. And it was so". (1:31). Maybe the shortage of plant-based food due to the environ-mental damage caused by the floods required for some animals to evolve into carnivores to survive, and a new eco-system that included plant-based and flesh-eating animals was created... Maybe?

This evolution is understandable and acceptable when it comes to animals because, unlike humans, they do not have the capacity to grow their own crops and are fully dependent on what is available to them. A balanced eco-system is imperative for their ongoing survival, it is a 'future insurance policy'.

However, such 'necessity' cannot be used by humans as an excuse for ongoing loss, abuse, and deterioration, because we have the capacity to grow our crops and restore vegetation.

Moses, by mean of his commandments, tried to restore in the Israelites (and humanity)[19] the realization of Oneness and to give the journey of awakening the awareness to its truth a 'kick start'.

---

[18]'duality' refers to separateness, to an us vs them attitude

[19]The Israelites are supposed to lead by example and be a 'light unto the nation'. When they restore the Oneness, they lead by example for all humanity.

Sadly, it seems that nothing much has changed or moved forward since then.

The attitudes of separateness and 'superiority' prevail today not only within humanity in general, but worse, within the Jewish People. Despite Moses' attempt to bring more compassion and minimize the consumption of animals and animal-based products, the majority of Jewish People still hold humans as separate from, and superior to, other living beings in a way that allows abusive dominion and makes it 'kosher'... This is the greatest Jewish failure of all, for it is a betrayal of the very core of Judaism, its realization of Oneness and its commitment for an ongoing awakening to this Oneness and to all it entails... It is out of alignment with Judaism.

It is not only the walls of slaughterhouses that need to be made of glass but the walls of the entire Animal Husbandry – meat, dairy, and egg industry, as well as wool, silk, and honey industries. But the walls are made of brick, and many human beings, including Jews, will continue to choose consuming flesh and other animal-based foods and products. It may take generations, if at all, for the truth of Oneness and all that it entails to be truly fully realised. Allowing this unfortunate truth, we Jews can be true and as per our commitment, journey towards the Oneness as much as we are able each day and each moment... We can allow this recognition of Oneness and compassion to lead us instead of the mistaken notion of superiority and abusive dominion... We will then remember that what serves our human desires are living, breathing, and feeling beings, and bring this awareness to guide us in the way we treat other life... By doing so, we will serve as a guide to others.

Rachel Angel-Sussman... 177

It is the least we can, and must, do if we are to stay true to Judaism, to our commitment to awaken to the truth of Oneness, and to our promise to serve 'as a light unto the nations'... Failing to do so leaves us with hollow practices and is a betrayal of Judaism and of our commitment and promise...Ultimately, it is a betrayal of the Source of life within us and without us.

Chapter 15:
Times and Seasons

Times and Seasons refers to the specific Holy Days in the Jewish Calendar. This theme which contains 35 commandments and related practices points to these special days, what they signify and advises how one is to celebrate them.

The Jewish seasons are truly beautiful; they not only remind us of the evolution of Judaism and the history of the Jewish People, they often also hold agricultural significance, and most importantly, they carry spiritual messages and remind us of our commitment to the ongoing journey to the Oneness.

The Commanded Festivals, their purpose, and their related practices

The commanded holy-days and festivals include:

Passover

Passover is a seven-day celebration marking the Jewish People escape from slavery in Egypt. Its central spiritual message is appreciation and gratitude for physical and spiritual freedom and what made this freedom possible. It also holds agricultural meaning, symbolising the arrival of Spring and the first crops.

The central commandments in Passover are:

- To celebrate and rejoice in the festival.
- To rest on the first and the last days of the seven days festival and not to work.
- Every male is to appear in the Sanctuary (a place of worship).
- Every person is to cleanse their home of all products containing yeast prior to the start of the festival and keep their home yeast free during the seven days of the festival. This is to commemorate the Israelites hasty escape from Egypt as they had no time to allow the bread to rise.
- Every household is to gather together and re-tell the story of the exodus in a particular order = Seder, to recount and pass on to the young the miracle of the exodus, the value of freedom and to express gratitude to the Source that made this freedom possible. It is customary to invite to one's Seder table anyone who is alone or unfortunate, for no one must be alone on the joy of Seder night.
  (Ex. 12:15-16 & 18-20; Ex. 13:3& 7-8; Ex. 23:14; Lev. 23:6-7-8; Deut.16:3, 14&16).

Shavuot and The Counting of the Omer (the first crop)

From Passover, the Israelites are commanded to count 49 days (seven weeks x seven days) - known as the 'counting of the Omer'. The 50th day is the festival of Shavuot (meaning 'weeks' in Hebrew) - A celebration of receiving the Torah which is believed to have been given to the Israelites on the 50th day following the exodus from Egypt. Shavuot is a day of joy and gratitude for the Torah.

The 49 days of counting the Omer are days of spiritual cleansing and preparation to receive the Torah and each day carries its own spiritual message. During the 49 days of counting the Omer, no celebrations, such as weddings, are allowed, the emphasis is on spiritual cleansing.

As with Passover, on Shavuot too one is commanded to celebrate and rejoice in the festival, to rest and not work, and every male is to attend the Sanctuary.

Like Passover, Shavuot too is an agricultural celebration of the fruits on the trees that are now beginning to bloom. To mark the festivity's agricultural significance, one is commanded to express gratitude for the products of the earth and eat only the fruit of the tree and dairy products, during Shavuot meat is not allowed.
(Ex 23:14; Lev. 23:15 & 21 Deut. 16:14 &16).

Sukkot

Sukkot is also a seven-day festival, and like Passover and Shavuot it has an historical, spiritual, and agricultural meaning.

Historically, it commemorates the protection of the Israelites during their 40year journey in the desert and the temporary dwellings that sheltered them during this journey.

It carries the spiritual meaning of gratitude.

Agriculturally, it is a harvest celebration as both crops and fruits are now ready for full harvesting.

The day following Sukkot – the eighth day -is *Simchat Torah* (Joy of Torah). The Israelites were commanded to read and study a chapter of the Torah each day, the eight day of Sukkot is the day when the yearly reading and study is completed and celebrated before it starts over once again.

As with Passover and Shavuot, on Sukkot also one is commanded to celebrate the festival and rejoice in it, to rest and not work on the first day and on the eighth day (Simchat Torah), and every male is to attend in the Sanctuary.

On Sukkot one is to build a Sukkah – a temporary dwelling under the stars where one is to eat and sleep for seven days to commemorate the Israelites temporary dwellings in the desert. As with Passover, it is customary to invite into one's Sukkah anyone who is alone, poor, or unfortunate, for it is a celebration of gratitude and abundance with crops and fruits ready for full harvesting. Gratitude for full harvesting is to be expressed by bringing to the Sukkah, holding and blessing 'The Four Kinds' which represent the four elements of the fruit of the earth: The Etrog (Citron), the Lulav (Palm Ford), the Hadassim (Myrtle Twig) and the Aravot (Willow Twigs).

On Simchat Torah one is also commanded to be merry and dance with the Torah books.
(Ex. 23:14; Lev. 23:35-36, 40 & 42, Deut. 16:14).

Rosh Hashana

The Jewish year is governed by the moon. Rosh Hashana celebrates the end of one year and the start of a new one. It expresses gratitude for the year that has passed with all its lessons, and joy and hope for a new beginning.

The commandments to rejoice, rest and not work apply.

Apart from celebrating with loved ones with a festive dinner that contains symbolic blessings for the new year, it is customary on Rosh Hashana to blow the Shofar (a trumpet made of a deer's horn) in the synagogue to symbolically open the gates of Heavens for the days of reflection and atonement that follow.
(Lev. 23:24-25; Num. 29:1).

Ten Days of Atonement and Yom Kippur

Following the celebration of *Rosh Hashana* the Israelites are commanded to enter ten days of self-reflection known as the *Ten Days of Atonement* – ten days of being at one with oneself, one's Soul and its source God/Source; of reflecting on the year that has passed with all its achievements and triumphs as its mistakes and misdemeanours; of asking for forgiveness wherever needed; and of offering forgiveness wherever needed.

The tenth day of atonement is *Yom Kippur* – A day of offering that concludes the process of reflection, forgiveness and making amends.

During the ten days of Atonement it is customary to go to the river or sea and empty one's pocket - a symbolic act of throwing away all that needs to be let go of to start anew.

On Yom Kippur one is commanded to fast from sundown to sundown, reflect and pray. The day concludes with blowing the Shofar once more.
(Lev. 23:27, 29, 31, 32).

The Shabbat

Shabbat is the sanctified seventh day of the week - a day of rest, gratitude, and connection to the Source Within (Soul) and Without (God) that marks the completion of the cycle of creation-evolution of life.

Shabbat (a day of rest) holds a universal importance and is valued by every path and every human, however, it holds a central place in Jewish life for alongside circumcision, it symbolises the covenant with, and the commitment to the ongoing journey of awakening to the Oneness of Source and all life.

While one works for six days to provide for oneself and one's earthly needs, the seventh day, Shabbat is sanctified as a day for the Soul.

Shabbat ensures that we do not work ceaselessly to accumulate more and more in greed or fear; that we do not take life in general, and our life in particular, for granted; and that we do not disconnect from the Source within (our Soul) and without (God).

It is a day of re-connection to the Source of Life and its flame within us (the Soul, the true Self); a day to reflect and express appreciation and gratitude for the fruit of our work, for our existence and for life itself, and for the Source of all life.

We are commanded to remember the Shabbat and sanctify it, to rest and not to work, and to refrain from travelling outside one's area of residence.
(Ex. 16:29; 20:8; 20:10; 23:12; 34:21).

The Mud Obscuring the Diamond of the Festivities

Jews in general, whether Orthodox, Traditional or Reform hold dear the festivals and Shabbat and adhere to them and to their related commandments. While some follow the commandments strictly and piously, others simply keep their related traditions, but despite various expressions, the underlying meaning of the festivals, the Shabbat, and the related commandments remain central.

Nevertheless, the beauty of the festivals and Shabbat is at times clouded by attitudes and behaviours that must be acknowledged and reflected on in the light of the 'guiding compass.'

The 'Mud' obscuring the Diamond of Passover

Clearing all yeast products from one's household has an historical significance we remember, honour, and commemorate the hardships experienced by the Israelites and we express gratitude for past protection and for present freedom.

Aside from its historical meaning, this commandment may also have hygienic significance. Passover is celebrated in Spring following the Winter hibernation. At a time when hygiene was not as easily attained as it is today, 'clearing one's house from yeast' provided a way to enforce a 'Spring Clean' – i.e. to clean one's home, utensils and storage facilities.

Today, the commandment of 'not eating and storing yeast' during Passover is honoured in different ways in different households.

In some households it is held very strictly, while in others more loosely. In some households all 'yeast products' are burned or thrown away, while in others one may 'seal' cupboards that contain them till the end of the festival, and in others, one may simply refrain from eating 'yeast products' as much as possible for the duration of the festival.

In some homes one cleans cupboards and exchanges everyday used pots, plates, utensils etc with 'Passover specific sets', in other homes one symbolically cleans and washes existing equipment, and in other homes, one may feel it unnecessary to fastidiously wash and clean yeast out of pots and utensils for they are always clean - Today we not only have good hygiene and dishes are continually washed after use, we also do not need to be prompted by Passover to do 'Spring Cleaning'.

None of these practices are a problem unless they become an end to themselves - a rigid 'must' rather than an offering... Because when they do, the home of someone who feels their home does not need 'cleaning', or who chooses to clean and wash their pots, plates, utensils etc rather than exchange and replace them - is deemed to be 'not kosher for Passover'... And the home of someone who chooses not to dispose of yeast products but rather put them aside in certain cupboards, or to simply refrain from using them as far as possible - is deemed to be 'not kosher for Passover'...

Consequently, those who adhere to 'exchanging' and 'sealing' not only scoff at those who do not, they also refrain from visiting them during the festive period... The result is division and exclusion.

The Israelites did not have 'Passover specific sets', surely washing and cleaning equipment and cupboards, or putting yeast aside, or even doing one's best, is just as honourable, effective and 'kosher.' Internal division and exclusion are not 'kosher', they are totally out of alignment with both the spirit of the Festival and with the spirit of Judaism.

Worse still, in the frantic adherence to 'no yeast', there is today a peculiar practice to use an unfathomable amount of disposable plastic plates, cutlery, cups etc that in a seven-day festival contribute to the world's pollution without mercy. This is neither aligned with the truth of Oneness and with the reverence for life and the planet that emanates from this truth, nor is it a behaviour that can serve as a model for others to follow.

The focus on the practice rather than its meaning results in something else being lost and it is time for reflection and change...

The 'Mud' obscuring the Diamond of Shabbat

Some of the commandments relating to Shabbat have unfortunately become a source of ongoing controversy and internal division in Jewish life and communities, and because the Festive holy-days share some of Shabbat's commandments, this controversy and division 'spills over' to them as well.

The underlying messages of Shabbat's commandments are clear and simple:

1. Remembering and sanctifying the Shabbat conveys the message that for six days we engage in attending to the needs of the body, on Shabbat we engage in what nurtures the Soul and its Source - A day where the mundane gives way to something higher.

2. Similarly, the commandment 'not to work' conveys the message that for six days we may engage in whatever work is needed to sustain ourselves, on Shabbat we relax, enjoy the product of our work and express gratitude and appreciation for the week's work as we reflect on its achievements and acknowledge any possible need to do better or differently.

3. The commandment 'to rest' does not mean 'doing nothing' (although one may choose to 'do nothing'). It means Shabbat is a day where 'shoulds' and 'musts' are put aside and replaced with restfulness, joy, inner peacefulness and the nurturing of one's Soul.

The commandments 'not to work' and 'to rest' apply not only for oneself but also to one's entire household including workers and working animals.

4. One is also commanded to refrain from travel outside one's area of residence. Travel meant engaging in work for one had to prepare one's tool of travel – being a carriage or similar - and one's working animal. Since work is not allowed on Shabbat and since working animals must also be rested, then one must refrain from unnecessary travel.

These are the guidelines for Shabbat and while they are clear, the detailed 'how to' is left open.

Every individual must listen within as to how to sanctify the Shabbat, how 'work' and 'rest' relate to them, and how to attend to their travel intentions, needs and boundaries. There is an underlying wisdom recognizing that what supports one person to sanctify the day and connect with their Soul and its Source, may not support another; what is mundane work for one is not for another; and how one finds restfulness and peace within is an individual matter.

But the possibility of individual variation seems to have threatened religious leaders (it may be that they feared a loss of spirit if the 'how to' is left to individuals). Consequently, Rabbis took upon themselves to decide on behalf of everyone the 'correct' way to sanctify the Shabbat, what 'work' and 'rest' mean, and the travel boundaries to put in place. Even though Rabbis did not – and still do not - agree with each other on these 'correct ways', their views were deemed 'the right way' or 'the wrong way' in their communities.

The problem is that while guidelines to practicing these commandments can be helpful, rigid prescriptions imposed by another are not.

Some of the 'prescribed' practices of Shabbat are beautiful and enhancing such as:

1. Marking the start of the Shabbat with the lighting of candles and prescribed blessings.
2. Marking the closure of Shabbat with the Havdalah service.
3. Baking special bread for the day, the Challah, to differentiate the mundane daily bread from Shabbat's bread.

Nevertheless, as beautiful and enhancing they may be, they are still 'prescribed' by someone, they may or may not work for everyone as a way of sanctifying the day - Room for individual variations must be left.

Some of the prescribed practices of Shabbat are not helpful, are out of context with our present time, and even with the spirit and intention of Shabbat...

1. We are told that there is one way to connect with our Soul and its Source (God) - via prayer, and moreover, prayer in the synagogue - and this is what one must do in Shabbat...

A 'must' which ignores two essential truths - First, while in the festivals of Passover, Shavuot and Sukkot males are commanded to appear in the sanctuary (synagogue), this is not a requirement for Shabbat.

Second, Temples and places of prayers are not needed for the benefit God's ego, they offer a sanctuary for whoever finds in them the peace to connect with their Soul and its Source - It is a beautiful way to connect but it is not the only way nor is it 'the way'... However, it seems that if someone connects with their Soul and its Source and finds nourishment, gratitude, and joy by basking in the sun on the beach, or attending to one's beloved garden, or having a picnic in nature with dear ones, or relaxing and having special time with one's loved ones to enjoy a movie, a sporting activity, or whatever else – it is not allowed, it is blasphemy, a sin.

2. Then there are the strict travel prohibitions...

Whether one's Soul calls them to express gratitude via prayer in the synagogue or elsewhere, one must not travel only walk – for travel is not allowed.

What if one is not able to walk? What if one is old, infirm, unwell, lives too far from the place of prayer or from any other place where they feel called to sanctify the day? – It seems that those who cannot walk, are excluded from the joy of the day...

What about young children or babies? They too must walk and even tots in prams cannot be pushed because the Rabbis decided this to be 'unallowable work'. Therefore, one either engages non-Jews to do what they are not allowed to do for themselves, or else one is excluded...

And what if it rains or is too hot to walk – Adults and children must walk rain or shine, and if one cannot cope with the weather, one is excluded...

The commandment 'not to travel outside the areas of one's residence' must be seen through the 'compass' of its time... It was given when people lived in close-knit communities, often in walled cities, sharing residential areas with family groups. Travel was needed either for work, or for pilgrimage (attending the Sanctuary) because sanctuaries were often constructed outside the community. Since on Shabbat one must rest and not work, and since one was not commanded to attend the sanctuary on Shabbat - there was no need for travel and Shabbat could be enjoyed in one's own community...

Today we do not live in walled cities, we do not live in one street or even in one suburb with our loved ones, we are lucky to live in the same city and our suburbs and cities are spread wide and far... One wonders what does 'area of residence' refer to? – to one's street, one's suburb, one's city?

The Torah writers offered helpful guidelines to the time with the central message being that Shabbat is about rest, gratitude, and connection, not about running around, hence, we need to be aware of the intention and boundaries of our travel on Shabbat. In an effort to re-create the conditions of bye-gone times, the Rabbis decided on Eruv – an imaginary walled area that includes some, but excludes most ... Whoever lives within these prescribed boundaries can share the joy of Shabbat together and whoever does not – be it parents, children, siblings, extended families or friends – is excluded from the joy of sharing Shabbat with loved ones as travel is forbidden... Creating such boundaries of 'areas of residence' in the fashion of thousands of years ago is not applicable to today's world. Surely one can see that dividing and separating communities and loved ones from one another is not in the spirit of Shabbat and indeed, not in the spirit of Judaism.

As for 'work' in relation to travel, what applied thousands of years ago, does not apply today. We no longer need to harness a carriage and a working animal... Most of us today have a comfortable means of transport for ourselves and we can also support others in their need for transport.

It may be time to use this commandment as a guide to use travel wisely, limit stressful unnecessary travel and ensure that our intentions are aligned with the spirit of Shabbat ...

Not only Shabbat is impacted by the travel limitations. According to the Rabbis these limitations apply also on the Festive Holy Days... However, the commandment of 'no travel outside one's areas of residence' was not prescribed for the festivals - only for Shabbat. This is not surprising as one was commanded to attend the sanctuary on the festivals, and this was only possible if one travelled... But the Rabbis insisted and their communities followed resulting in the isolation and exclusion of many, including loved ones, not only on Shabbat, but also during the festivals – when parents, children, siblings, families and friends are meant to rejoice together. This is not in the spirit of the Festivals or Judaism.

It is not only 'travel' that is out of context. The 'must not do' list both out of and within one's home contains a host of rules given by the Rabbis as to what 'work' consists of and the 'right and only way' to sanctify the Shabbat and the Festivals...

3. Outside the home - Even walking within the prescribed boundaries – The Eruv - is not barrier free... If one needs to cross a busy road on the way to the synagogue (as is often the case in today's cities), one cannot press the crossing button as it is classified as 'work', so unless one is willing to risk their life, they need to ask someone else (a non-Jew) to do it for them... Surely it is better to cross the road safely than risk one's life, and if it is ok to ask another to do it for us, why is it not ok for us to do it for ourselves?

4. Within the home - If one wants to turn the light on, if one is cold and needs to turn on a heater, or hot and needs to turn on a cooler, or needs to warm a meal - one cannot because all these according to the Rabbis is 'work of the mundane' and 'lighting a fire' (which was forbidden on Shabbat, Ex 35;1-3). Consequently, one 'must' utilize a computerized switch or otherwise sit in darkness, in the cold or the heat, and with a cold meal...

The prohibition to 'light fire' on Shabbat related specifically to building the tabernacles and its furnishing - a construction requiring melting metals in fire. The message was simply that no construction work was allowed on Shabbat... Also, in the context of time, lighting a fire was a complex and demanding affair, for one had to collect wood, chop it, light the fire, and replenish it. The Israelites were told not to engage in such strenuous work on Shabbat and the Festivals. They had to prepare the wood and fire before the Shabbat/ Festivals, so that it lasts through the night and day... Since it is ok to utilize a computerized switch, it is obvious that having the comfort of light or warmth etc is not the issue but rather the 'work'... But we live in a world where we no longer need to gather and chop wood - turning a switch is not 'work'.

More still, if one lives on the fourth floor, one is not allowed to press the lift button, so unless the lift can be put on auto-pilot, one must either walk four flight of stairs, or ask someone else (non-Jew) to press the lift button for them... If one cannot manage the stairs and has no one to press the lift button for them – one is compelled to stay indoors – more isolation, more exclusion... Since it is ok to travel in the lift on auto-pilot, surely it is ok to press the button ourselves, and surely it is better to press a lift button than to damage the joyful spirit of Shabbat and the Festivals and remain isolated.

These are but a few examples of the imposed limitations resulting in exclusion, and damaging the spirit of Shabbat, the festivals, and the spirit of Judaism... There is nothing wrong with anyone choosing to follow the rules as prescribed by the Rabbis, if this is their wish, their Soul calling and their way of connecting and finding restfulness and peace in Shabbat and the Festivals - Problems arise not from the practices themselves but when:

- Practices become rigid rules rather than guides and are adhered to in a black and white fashion indiscriminately.
- Practices become the end rather than the means to a deeper message, and are seen to be the 'only right way' to express and live the message.

- We ask someone else to do for us that which we deem to be 'wrong' to do ourselves.
- One attempts to enforce them on others as a condition for inclusion.
- One judges anyone who chooses to sanctify Shabbat and the Festivals differently using the commanded guidelines as per their Soul's calling, as not being 'Shomer Shabbat' (not preserving the Shabbat') and not preserving the festivals.

Then, even if unintentionally, they become nothing but rigid prescriptions resulting in division from, and exclusion of, others including loved ones.

This is the unfortunate reality in Judaism today in relation to Shabbat and the festivals, the 'mud' obscuring the beautiful diamond. It is out of line with the spirit of Oneness, with the spirit of Judaism... All due to the failure to differentiate practices from their underlying message, and to hold the commandments in the light of the 'guiding compass' of alignment with the context of time and with the truth of Oneness and the beauty and moral precept that entails from this truth.

It is time to awaken...

Epilogue

Many years ago, on one of my visits to my beloved country of birth - Israel - on a beautiful sunny Saturday, my husband and I took our two young daughters to Tel Aviv beach. We wanted to bask in the sun, play in the waves, be nurtured, and allow our Souls to express gratefulness for life and its Source - the Source of which we are part.

As we walked joyfully, a woman with a little boy - no more than four - passed us, they were on the way to the synagogue. As they neared us the little boy looked at us, I smiled at him noticing the longing in his eyes... Then I heard him dare ask his mother: "Mummy, why are we never allowed to go to the beach on Saturday?" His mother gave him a scornful look, then looked at us angrily, even though I gave her a smile, and pointing a finger to her little boy she answered: "What do you think God wants you to do on Shabbat? - Go to the beach or to the synagogue and pray?" The little boy was silent, he looked down with shame, and my heart sank. I cannot imagine what he thought of God – the Source of the Life Force Energy; I cannot imagine what he thought of himself for he is part of this Source, part of this Life Force Energy; I cannot begin to imagine what 'story' he created at that moment in time. And I promised myself that one day I will answer him.

Today is this 'one day'...

This little boy is a man now, probably a father himself, maybe even a grand-father, and unless he found the courage to dare to continue asking, I suspect that he gave his children and grand-children the very same answer that his mother once gave him... But today I want to give him and all the little children an answer, whether they dare to ask or not:

Yes little one, you can go to the beach, or the woods, or down the river, or wherever else your Soul calls you to sing, praise, pray and express your love and gratitude on Shabbat and the Festivals.

You can because there are many ways to sanctify Shabbat and Festivals and many places where they can be sanctified. There are many ways for you to connect with your Soul and its Source and express your love and gratitude and many places where connection can take place.

You can because 'work' means something different to each of us - what is mundane and a chore to me, may be an expression of joy and gratitude to you, and vice versa... What brings me inner peace, restfulness and connection may not bring you the same and vice versa.

You can because no one but you and I must decide how to sanctify Shabbat and the Festivals, and how to follow the commandments of 'do not work', 'rest', and 'refrain from travel'. Listen within and you will be guided... And allow others to do the same for themselves.

Little one, there is nothing wrong with you going to the synagogue on Shabbat and the Festivals if this is the calling of your Soul – Go, sing, praise and pray to your heart's and Soul's content and express your love and gratitude.

There is also nothing wrong with you choosing to follow the Rabbis instructions for Shabbat and the Festivals if this answers your Soul's calling – Do so with joy...

But remember that it is someone's interpretation and prescription and do not follow without awareness and discrimination.

Remember that whatever the interpretation and prescription, it is not 'the only right way'... That any interpretation and practice is an expression of a certain commandment and each commandment is an expression of a certain message - and it is this message that is of the essence, not the practice itself and there possibly are many equally beautiful and valid expressions for this message.

Remember to check each commandment and the prescribed practice chosen to express it, in the light of the 'guiding compass' – the 'compass' of the intended message, of the context of time, and most importantly, the 'compass' of alignment with the truth of Oneness... For if it does not align with the Oneness of all life, it is most likely an 'imposter', 'mud' that covers the diamond of Judaism.

Remember that whatever interpretation and prescription you choose, it is not OK to ask another to do for you what you choose not to do for yourself.

And know that forgetting all of this will result in division and exclusion, in undue judgement of anyone (including yourself) when the calling of their (or your) Soul differs, and in the loss of the truth of Oneness - the spirit of Judaism.

So yes little boy, you can go to the beach on Saturday and on the Festival holy-days, you can let your little body bask in the sun, feel the sand and the water and the breeze... You can let your Soul sing gratitude to its Source and the Source of all life - the Source that is within you, the Source that you are... This is the Spirit of Shabbat, of the Festivals, of Judaism.

For Judaism is simply a commitment to awaken your awareness to the truth of Oneness, the truth of unity of all life, and the beauty, goodness and moral precept emanating from these truths... It is allowing the commitment to these truths shine in your heart and be your true inner voice... It is having commandments that when seen for their messages, in the context of time, and in alignment with the compass of Oneness, can remind you, support you, and aid you to re-connect if you are lost... It is being the best version of yourself each day, and giving your best each day, shinning within and without and being 'a model' unto others.

Judah Al-Harizi (c.1170-1235), a medieval Jewish poet, said that Judaism is like a tree whose roots are in heaven but its branches reaching down to earth and creating an abundance of 'Judaisms'. This is Judaism my way, and I pray also, Judaism your way and Judaism the way of each of my fellow Jews...

I believe this to be true not only for Judaism but for every offered path - be it Christianity, Islam, Buddhism, Hinduism, or whatever other path - For this is religion my way...

Acknowledgement

My sincere thanks to Leah Bangma. Her tireless efforts and support played an important part in bringing this book into being.

I also thank my husband Peter Sussman for his patience and for his contribution to title the book.

Bibliography

Religion and Judaism From A Different Perspective is not a 'research project'. It is founded on personal experience and personal realization. It is born from within and not from without, consequently its main resources are the Holy Scripture, the Commandments, and the Author herself – Rachel Angel-Sussman.

Nevertheless, some voices touched the author and must be mentioned.

1. *The Holy Scripture*, Koren Publishers, Jerusalem, 1989 Edition.

2. www.judaism101/whatdojewsbelieve/613 commandments Copyright @ 5756-5771 (1995-2019) Tracey R. Rich.

3. Rachel Angel-Sussman, To Life, A journey of Home Coming and Re-discovering Our Self and Our Humanity, Copyright @ 2015 by Rachel Angel-Sussman, published by Xlibris.

4. Brother David Stein Rast, *Mystical Core of Organized Religion*, New Realities Vol X, No 4, March/April 1990, pp 35-37.

5. Article by Rabbi Jeffrey B. Kamins, *On Ethical Eating*, June 2017

6. Jonathan Kirsche, *The Untold Story of the Jewish People – The Woman Who Laughed at God*, Vicking Compass, a member of Penguin Putman Inc, 2001.

7. Rhonda Byrne *The Secret* Atria Books of Simon & Schuster Inc, 2006